Interactive Exercises
for the **Police Recruit**
Assessment Process

Succeeding at Role Plays

Interactive Exercises for the **Police Recruit Assessment Process**

Succeeding at Role Plays

Richard Malthouse
Peter Kennard
Jodi Roffey-Barentsen

LearningMatters

Acknowledgements

The authors would like to thank the following people for their help in the writing of this book: Nazan Djemal, Sachvinder Kaur Mahal, Ela Wesolowska and Ziggy Wesolowski.

First published in 2009 by Learning Matters Ltd

British Library Cataloguing in Publication Data
A CIP record for this book is available from the British Library.

ISBN: 978 1 84445 249 1

Cover design by Topics – The Creative Partnership
Text design by Code 5 Design Associates Ltd.
Project Management by Diana Chambers
Typeset by Kelly Gray
Printed and bound in Great Britain by TJ International Ltd., Padstow, Cornwall

Learning Matters Ltd
33 Southernhay East
Exeter EX1 1NX
Tel: 01392 215560
info@learningmatters.co.uk
www.learningmatters.co.uk

Contents

Introduction to the Interactive Exercises

Introduction

Interactive exercises, also referred to as role plays, are an important part of the Police and PCSO recruitment process and appear to be the thing candidates worry about the most. This is because most people never get to do one and, more importantly, they don't actually know what to do; it is the fear of the unknown. This book takes away that fear. It concentrates on just the interactive exercises. It describes in detail how to prepare yourself mentally and physically; outlines the process and set tasks; offers interactive exercises for you to practise; and assists you in analysing the content.

What is an interactive exercise or role play exactly? It is a contrived situation in which people interact with each other and act out the role of specified characters. Frequently it is used to enable a person to understand another's point of view or to behave in a way that is perhaps counter to their own values. However, within the context of the assessment centre it is used as a test to see how you are able to interact in given situations. The interactive exercise tests your ability to:

- communicate;

- ask open and closed questions appropriately;

- take control of situations;

- make decisions;

- take responsibility;

- be fair;

- be impartial;

- challenge inappropriate behaviour.

Ideally you will use this book with a friend or colleague, with this person taking on the role of the actor. However, it is still of value to work through the contents on your own. It is recognised that the assessors at the assessment centre are fully trained and this cannot be emulated by the person volunteering to take the part of the role actor for you. However, this is a necessary compromise and practising the experience can be very beneficial. Human nature may play a part in your wish to appear to do well in front of your friends, peers or members of your family. You may be tempted to take a peek at the suggested questions, so as not to lose face or appear silly. But you will gain far more from this book if you resist the temptation.

Remember, the process of learning means that you will make lots of mistakes. Learn from them and look at mistakes as learning opportunities.

The seven core competencies

You will be assessed against competencies that are relevant to the role of a police officer. What is a competency? A competency is a statement of how something should be done or performed, for example, *Makes sure that customers are satisfied with the service they receive.* It is observable and measurable and can be achieved by you by simply asking, *Are you happy with what I am proposing or is there anything else I can assist you with?*

When you are assessed, consideration will be given to *what* you do and *how* you do it. Assessors will watch you and give marks as you complete the exercises. They will consider your performance in relation to the seven core competencies. These are listed below along with a brief explanation of each (Cox, 2007).

1. Respect for race and diversity

Considers and shows respect for the opinions, circumstances and feelings of colleagues and members of the public, no matter what their race, religion, position, background, circumstances, status or appearance.

2. Team working

Develops strong working relationships inside and outside the team to achieve common goals. Breaks down barriers between groups and involves others in discussions and decisions.

3. Community and customer focus

Focuses on the customer and provides high-quality service that is tailored to meet their individual needs.

Understands the communities that are served and shows an active commitment to policing that reflects their needs and concerns.

4. Effective communication

Communicates ideas and information effectively, both verbally and in writing.

Uses language and a style of communication that is appropriate to the situation and people being addressed.

Makes sure that others understand what is going on.

5. Problem solving

Gathers information from a range of sources.

Analyses information to identify problems and issues and makes effective decisions.

6. Personal responsibility

Takes personal responsibility for making things happen and achieving results.

Displays motivation, commitment, perseverance and conscientiousness.

Acts with a high degree of integrity.

7. Resilience

Shows resilience, even in difficult circumstances.

Is prepared to make difficult decisions and has the confidence to see them through.

(Cox, 2007, p10)

3

The purpose of an interactive exercise

The interactive exercise consists of placing you in a given situation where you are assessed on your ability to deal with it. It is designed to identify how you are able to read and understand written instructions and how you then interact, communicate and transact with others. It will test your ability to comprehend a situation and how you are able to adopt an appropriate response to it.

You will be dealing with just one role actor, although another person will be in the room to assess how you do. Occasionally, there may be two other people in the room, but they will be there for the purpose of ensuring that the marking is fair and consistent.

Prior to attending the assessment centre, you will be provided with a Centre Welcome Pack. You will be given the role of Customer Service Officer; your responsibilities are listed within this document and include:

- ensuring that the customers at the shopping centre are provided with a very high level of customer service; this is also provided to people visiting the centre;
- being given, to investigate and to sort out, complaints from discontented customers, visitors and staff working at the centre;
- producing accurate reports of incidents and events in writing;
- offering resolutions to problems;
- offering advice to staff and customers in respect of the shopping centre's equal opportunities policy;
- maintaining safe working practices within the centre;
- offering a range of customer services to customers and visitors to the centre, such as:
  - dealing with some of the more serious problems that may arise;
  - helping Customer Service Assistants with various lost property;
  - providing information;
  - dealing with lost children and returning them to a responsible adult;
  - liaising between the management and customers for all customer services-type problems.

(Adapted from National Policing Improvement Agency, 2007, p5)

It is recommended that you familiarise yourself with the contents of the pack prior to attending the assessment centre.

You will be given four interactive exercises; each is split into two five-minute parts, with a 90-second interval. The first part will be the preparation phase and the second, the activity stage, where you will meet a role actor. The scenarios occur within what is a typical shopping centre, which we will refer to as the Eastshire Shopping Centre.

Typically, the types of situation you will be called to deal with are as follows.

- A customer who wishes to discuss an incident that occurred at the Eastshire Shopping Centre.

- An employee within the Eastshire Shopping Centre, who wishes to discuss an incident that occurred there.

- A customer who wishes to discuss a security issue at the Eastshire Shopping Centre.

- An employee who wishes to discuss a security issue at the Eastshire Shopping Centre.

The preparation stage

During the preparation stage you will be given written information that is relevant to the exercise you are about to undertake. You will be given a desk in a room with five minutes to study the information and prepare for the next part, the activity stage.

You can make notes on the paper supplied and you are permitted to use them in the activity stage. The instructions are left where you found them. However, it is good practice not to rely on too many notes. If you do, you may discover that you are unlikely to be able to find what you are looking for during the role play. As a coping strategy, try to commit the salient information to memory. If there are a lot of facts and figures, then note these down on only one side of paper; use notes sparingly.

It is not unusual for candidates to forget who it is they are supposed to be speaking to. Often the names of people are confused, for example, the name of the person making a complaint is exchanged with the name of the person being complained about or discussed. To avoid this, write down the names of the people concerned and in particular the name of the person who you are going to be talking to.

While you are preparing, think about what is actually described in front of you. Do not assume and do not make up any further information that does not exist. If you feel you will need to enquire further, make a mental note of it and be sure to ask when you go into the room. Remember that it is very unlikely that you have been given all the information that relates to the interactive exercise. Your task is to think about what else you want to know and then write it down in bullet form.

Stay in what is called the 'Here and Now'. In other words, don't project what you think might happen, because it might not. Your mind works in such a way that it does not like gaps. If it does find a gap, your brain will often try to fill it for you, and this can be done subconsciously. If you think about it, from the point at which you have read all that you have been given, the possible paths are almost limitless. If you start imagining what is going to happen, the chances are that you will be wrong and that could influence your performance.

Sometimes students do what is known as scripting. This is where, based on the information they have been given, they decide what they are going to say. They then decide what will be said in response and then what they will say in return. Our advice is simple: don't script the whole conversation that you think may occur, because it probably will not work out like that. When your five minutes are over, a buzzer will sound and you will make your way to the outside of the activity room. You will not be assessed on the preparation stage; you will not be permitted to take anything with you other than your notes. You may feel nervous at this stage, and that's a good thing as it will make you sharper and more able to think. Remember, you can do this; all you have to do is talk to someone in order to:

- find out what the issue is;

- find out what they would like to happen; and

- decide on your course of action.

Think about what you are going to say as your first introductory sentence. Are you going to introduce yourself? Are you going to make sure you know who you are talking to? If you were the person you are going to meet, what would you want from you?

There will be a period of 90 seconds between the end of the preparation and the start of the interactive exercise. Don't worry though, as you will be guided where to go. When the next buzzer sounds you are on! You go in, scan the room and make your way towards the role actor.

The activity stage

In this stage you will interact in your role as the newly appointed Customer Service Officer. You will do this for five minutes with a trained role actor. There will also be an assessor present.

In each exercise the role actor may be male or female; the information you are given in the preparation stage will take this into account. When you see the person they will be wearing a name badge to help you identify them.

The role actor will normally have a sentence to say to you as an opening line. After that, the onus is on you to take the initiative. The role actor will respond to you with a set of predefined responses. Normally, they will have up to 20 set responses. Do not expect this to be like a normal conversation. The person will respond to you but don't expect them to interact with you using small talk. There is no magic phrase either, such as 'So tell me all I need to know' – they will not. You are going to have to work for information, so consider what you want to establish and don't be afraid to ask apparently obvious questions.

Never Assume!

You will no doubt have heard that to assume makes an ass out of you and me.

Ass U Me

So try never to assume.

Listen to what is being said. If you have asked a question, it would be silly not to listen to the reply, but candidates are often too busy thinking about the next question, rather than listening to the answer they are being given. That is a pity, because it is likely that the role actor will be communicating something of importance.

Respond to what has been said. Confirm what you believe has been said by paraphrasing, for example 'So what you are saying is that this has happened on a number of occasions to the same individual and you want something done about it?' You can ask them what they want, for example 'What would you like me to do about this exactly?' Often the answer will not be the most useful, but at least you are looking at the situation from their perspective.

If you are fortunate, the reply may represent a critical aspect of the role play. Listen to them and consider their point of view. If you are considering something, SAY IT! You cannot be given marks for thinking things – only vocalising them.

The Magnificent Seven

During the interactive exercise you may feel that you are getting tied in knots or can't think what to ask next, or even that you are repeating yourself. Remember, you have five minutes for this exercise and a lot of clues given to you in the preparation stage. They are not trying to catch you out. You are told what the situation is and now you are expected to deal with it. This will require some investigation, and for this we can use the Magnificent Seven.

These are seven words that can make your life much easier when you are attempting to gain information from another person. They are:

1. What?

2. When?

3. Where?

4. Why?

5. Who?

6. Which?

7. How?

These words are the tools of the Customer Service Officer, who can use them as a key to unlock the available information. For example, you can ask the following questions.

- What happened?

- When did it happen?

- Where was this?

- Why was that?

- Who was involved?

- Which one was it?

- How did it happen?

Open and closed questions

A question can be described as being open or closed. A closed question will elicit very little in the way of information. For example:

- Is your coat long and dark brown?

- Did you go out yesterday?

- Were you at work yesterday?

- Is your car a Ford?

- Did you have a full English breakfast?

You will notice that a suitable response could be either 'yes', 'no' or 'I don't know'. If you are attempting to find out more than that, the closed question is not very useful. During the role plays, you should only ask closed questions if you want to establish that what has been discussed is correct, or you are trying to confirm a statement or fact. For example:

Candidate:
'So you are saying the dog is a chocolate-brown Labrador, its name is Lillie and it was last seen yesterday at 10.30 a.m. running up the road after the postlady on her bike?'

Role actor:
'Yes.'

There is nothing wrong with using closed questions, but where people go wrong is using them at the wrong time. If you think about types of questions being like tools, you want to use the right tool for the job. When you go into the role play it would be appropriate to use lots of open questions; later you can use the closed ones to confirm what you believe you know.

Open questions, on the other hand, are used to elicit information that is not known to the questioner. In general, they tend to elicit more in the way of a response. For example, here the closed questions referred to earlier have been made into open questions.

Closed		Open
Is your coat long and dark brown?	becomes	Describe your coat to me.
Did you go out yesterday?	becomes	What did you do yesterday?
Were you at work yesterday?	becomes	Where were you yesterday?
Is your car a Ford?	becomes	What type of car do you have?
Did you have a full English breakfast?	becomes	What did you have for breakfast exactly?

Open questions enable you to ask about things of which you have no knowledge. When you are talking to the role actor, you are trying to get into their world. Often you will have an idea from the information that was given to you at the start of the exercise, but there will always be more to find out.

If you were to ask a person about their lunch and only asked closed questions, it would mean that you could easily miss something. For example, if the person you are questioning had unusual eating habits and their favourite pizza topping was pepperoni and Marmite, by asking only closed questions you would be unlikely to find this out. This is because, if you hadn't suspected a pepperoni and Marmite topping, you would not have asked about it. The open question, on the other hand, can take you into the world of the other person, for example:

'A pizza, you say; what was on that pizza?'
Response: 'Pepperoni and Marmite.'

Another advantage of open questions is that they are also less time-consuming than closed questions. For example, a closed question would ask:

- 'Is your jumper brown?' Response, 'No.'

- 'Is your jumper red?' Response, 'No.'

- 'Is your jumper blue?' Response, 'No.'

- 'Is your jumper green?' Response, 'No.'

- 'Is your jumper grey?' Response, 'No.'

- 'Is your jumper yellow?' Response, 'Yes.'

The open question would ask:

- 'What colour is your jumper?' Response, 'Yellow.'

By thinking about what you want to find out and constructing the question in an appropriate way, you will be able to illicit all the information you need to deal with the role play in the desired way.

Like closed questions, open questions have their time and that is when you wish to identify the shape, size and nature of the problem you are facing. Remember, you cannot deal with a problem until you have identified what that problem is. An appropriate mix of open and closed questions used at the right time will help you identify the problem you face.

TED PIE

After you have asked about something for a while, there is a possibility you could start repeating yourself, for example 'Tell me about the room', 'Tell me about the lady', 'Tell me about the locker'.

There is something you can use to make your interaction with others more meaningful and less repetitive. What you need is a slice of TED PIE.

TED PIE is a mnemonic in which each first letter is representative of a question:

Tell me	Precisely
Explain to me	In detail
Describe to me	Exactly

Using these words in combination enables you to ask questions of others that are both meaningful and to the point.

For example, you could ask:

Tell me	Precisely
Explain to me	In detail
Describe to me	Exactly

9

'Tell me exactly what happened.'

Tell me	Precisely
Explain to me	In detail
Describe to me	Exactly

'Describe to me in detail what was said.'

Tell me	Precisely
Explain to me	In detail
Describe to me	Exactly

'Describe to me precisely what you did.'

(Taken from TED PIE course handout, The Interview Success Company Ltd, © 2009)

Practise these techniques, with your family, friends, colleagues or partner. By doing this they will soon become easier. Then you will have less to think about in the assessment centre!

The resources available to you

Sometimes candidates find themselves stuck because they are unaware of what support or assistance they can offer in terms of people, equipment, vehicles, etc. As you know, you are offered an information pack about two weeks before you attend the assessment centre. It is recommended that you get to know this material well. The trouble is that you may find yourself in some situations where you want to offer support, but are not sure what you can offer.

To contextualise, let's say, for example, that a person is parking where they should not. Through a series of questions and answers, you establish that the reason they are parking where they do is because they are taking a large amount of money to the bank and they want to get as close to the bank as possible; it is an issue of their personal safety. So what can you offer? In short, the answer is anything you like (within reason). You could offer a parking space in the centre and a couple of security guards to escort the person safely to the bank. You could arrange for the person to be picked up by security and escorted to the bank in a car or have the route lined with security officers! The example is being exaggerated to make the point that you should not restrict your actions because you are unaware of the resources available to you; the world is your oyster.

Equal opportunity and diversity

Aspects of equal opportunity and diversity may impact on your performance. Sometimes there is confusion about these terms. Equal opportunity is about giving people the same opportunities, while diversity is treating people according to their individual needs. To describe this, it is useful to think of a race. If everybody had an equal opportunity, everyone would be at the start line. However, in life not everyone is standing at the start line; some people are behind it and a long way off. The race may well be over by the time they have reached the start line. The reasons for this are many and varied, but, to give you an idea in very broad terms, we can consider the following.

- English as a second language – they could not read the instructions so were unaware that the race was being held today at this location.

- People with disabilities – they were not able to read the flyers as their sight was impaired; they too may have to rely on other methods of communication; unfortunately only flyers were used on this occasion.

- Single parents – they dearly wanted to be in the race, but they could not give up enough time to train and as a consequence may not perform to their best. What is more, one of the children is ill and so they can't make it as the childminder is unavailable – probably running in the race themselves.

- Religious reasons – the race is being held during Ramadan. The fasting means that this person may feel unable to run at their best today – perhaps next time, if it's held at a more suitable time.

- The person is transsexual – other people are complaining that they don't want them using the changing rooms with them and 'What about the toilet facilities – we can't have a man in the ladies' toilet, can we?' This person chose not to turn up to the race at all.

In an effort to be fair, sometimes people are offered the same rules, but sometimes the same rules for everyone may not be fair.

The six strands of diversity

Diversity is described under six strands, namely:

1. race

2. gender

3. disability

4. sexual orientation

5. age

6. religion.

Race

This includes race, colour, nationality and ethnic or national origins. It is unlawful for a person to discriminate on racial grounds against another person. The discrimination can be direct, indirect, victimisation or harassment.

Gender

This refers to being a woman, a man or a transsexual, whether married, not married or in a civil partnership. Discrimination is sometimes directed towards individuals because of their gender.

Disability

The disability can be physical, sensory or mental. Examples of these, respectively, are cancer, diabetes, multiple sclerosis and heart conditions; hearing or sight impairments, or a significant mobility difficulty; and mental health conditions or learning difficulties. Discrimination is sometimes directed towards individuals because of their disability.

Sexual orientation

This includes being attracted to people of the same sex, people of the opposite sex, or people of both sexes. Both-sex attraction is called bisexuality. The word 'bisexual', or occasionally just 'bi', is used to describe people who are attracted to both sexes. Homophobia is an irrational fear or hatred of homosexuals or homosexuality, and can result in prejudice against gay members of the community.

Age

The clue is in the title, but it generally includes situations where a person has been treated less favourably on the basis of their age, without justification. This may be because they are considered too young or too old.

Religion

You have a right to have your own religious beliefs or other philosophical values comparable to a religion. You also have the right to have no religion or belief. Major religions that are generally recognised include:

- Buddhism
- Christianity
- Hinduism
- Islam
- Judaism
- Rastafarianism
- Sikhism.

People can be discriminated against simply because other people do not like their religion, and sometimes this intolerance can be traced back over hundreds of years. Other examples of discrimination in relation to religion are where a person is not afforded time and space for prayer, or where the person, who prefers to dress in a certain way to cover parts of their body, is not offered a job because of this preference.

Respect for diversity

Considerations of diversity go beyond the legislation; having respect for diversity means accepting that not everyone is just like you. It means taking time and effort to consider what life is like for others. In general terms, it means treating other people as you would like to be treated yourself. Many people have experienced bullying at some time in their lives, often as children, but it doesn't stop just because you become an adult. Often it becomes more subtle, for others less subtle and, in extreme cases, unfortunately violent.

The type of behaviour that is no longer tolerated is generally associated with the derogatory words some people use to describe others, the looks they may give, the humour they share and the things they choose to do or not to do. This behaviour is inappropriate.

When to challenge inappropriate behaviour

If you are considering applying for the police, you won't be a racist. Recognising racist behaviour when people are being openly racist is easy and, if witnessed, should be stopped. The difficulty arises when it is subtle or done as a result of ignorance. How could you differentiate between the two? The answer is simple: in either case, if the behaviour appears inappropriate, you need to challenge it.

Racist behaviour has been used in this book to emphasise the point being discussed, but the points raised are pertinent to all six strands of diversity. What, though, is inappropriate? This is a difficult question to answer because, where do you draw the line? If you see a certain behaviour and feel the need to question whether that behaviour is appropriate, it probably is not. The terms used can include a reference to a group of people based on their ethnic origin coupled with a derogatory statement, normally a generality, for example, 'They're all the same those thieving [specific group]', or 'It's typical of those [specific group] – they take the houses and the jobs; what about us?'

What about gender? For example, 'Look, if we give her the job, she'll be off on maternity leave in no time and who's going to pay for it? Us, that's who.'

What about religion? For example, 'That's all very well, but she'll be spending all day on her hands and knees pointing to Mecca. We've got work to do.'

All of these represent inappropriate behaviour and, as such, should be challenged.

Respect for race and diversity is tested during the interactive exercises. On occasion you may hear something similar to the examples given above. You recognise that challenging the behaviour is appropriate, but how do you actually challenge someone?

It goes like this:

> **Role actor**: 'You see it's not the first time I have had dealings with these low-life Romanian beggars.'
>
> **Candidate**: 'Let me stop you there. I don't like the way you are describing them as low-life. I must challenge your assumptions; please don't use that term again.'

or

> **Role actor**: 'You know she's the team leader, but, not unlike many other women I could mention, she's useless at her job.'
>
> **Candidate**: 'I must challenge that. I don't appreciate the way in which you are generalising women negatively; please don't do it again.'

or

> **Role actor**: 'You can take the man out of the jungle, but you can't take the jungle out of the man.'

> **Candidate**: 'Your behaviour is totally unacceptable. I don't like it. The company has a policy against it. Please stop your racist behaviour.'

Generally, the behaviour exhibited within the role play will not be as obvious as the examples above; you will find these within the interactive exercises later in this book. The mistake many candidates make is not stepping in there and then to make a challenge. A candidate may fail to challenge a statement and nods in agreement. If you do this, the inference will be that you are in agreement with the person. As a result, you could fail the assessment within the competency, Respect for Race and Diversity. Alternatively, a candidate may recognise the inappropriate behaviour but waits until the person stops talking to get in, as they see interrupting as being rude. Unfortunately, by the time they get around to the challenge, something else has come up that they now start to deal with; the moment has gone and the opportunity for challenge has been lost. Again, if there is no challenge given it is likely that you will fail under the competency, Respect for Race and Diversity.

What can you do to prepare?

You can start preparing now by listening to the words people are using when describing others. Ask yourself, if you were in the assessment centre, would a challenge be appropriate? Having done this, consider your own behaviour. Are the words you use appropriate? Could the everyday sayings or phrases you use be subject to misinterpretation or are they simply inappropriate? Sometimes people inherit inappropriate sayings that are almost embedded in the subconscious. For example, you may think back to the things your grandparents may have said; although not regarded as inappropriate at the time, if we were to utter such things today we may be committing a criminal offence – yes, times have changed.

Reflective practice

The following pages are dedicated to you practising the interactive exercise. After you have completed each one, undertake what is referred to as reflective practice. You can do this by asking yourself four things:

1. What did I do?

2. How well did I do it?

3. What does this book say I should have done?

4. What will I do differently in future?

Having identified these you can devise an Action Plan.

You can find the form below to do this (if it helps you can photocopy it to use). You don't need anyone else to tell you how you did, as the beauty of reflective practice is that you know how well you did and, if you are honest with yourself, you will know in which areas you need to do more work.

Question 3 above can be easily answered. At the end of each interactive exercise suggested questions are listed for the purposes of feedback. Comparing these to your own efforts will benefit you and prepare you for doing even better on the next occasion.

Reflective Practice Sheet

Title	Your observations
1. What did I do?	
2. How well did I do it?	
3. What does this book say I should have done?	
4. What will I do differently in future?	Desired outcome:
5. Action Plan	S M A R T

Reflective practice is all about taking responsibility for your own efforts in an attempt to improve whatever it is you are doing. You are the person who knows best what you can do well and what needs improving, so arguably it is you who is best placed to decide what requires improvement.

You will notice from the Reflective Practice Sheet that the reflective process consists of four parts or phases. The first part asks 'What did I do?' Thinking about what happened is always a good place to start the process. At this stage you think about the role play, remembering as much as you can about it. For example, you could ask yourself:

- 'Did I introduce myself?'
- 'Did I listen to the role actor?'
- 'Did I listen more than I talked?'
- 'Did I stop to recap?'
- 'Did I get stuck?'
- 'Did I feel that I had messed it up?'

As you ask these questions, try to remember how you felt as you approached each part of the role play. The feeling that you have messed it up is a common one. Sometimes you may feel that you have made a mistake and feel that you have failed the assessment. The analogy is a little like taking your driving test where you make a mistake. You feel sure that you have failed and, as a result, your driving deteriorates, your concentration drops and you chastise yourself for being such an idiot. But, at that moment, you had not failed. Unfortunately, your driving is poor due to you being so hard on yourself and you are in danger of failing. Why? Because you have decided you have – there is no other reason than that. There is the danger of creating a self-fulfilling prophecy. The same can happen in the assessment centre where you make a mistake and you cannot put it behind you. If you dwell on it you will disadvantage yourself. The best policy is to put the experience behind you and move on, having learned from it.

The second part of the process considers the question 'How well did I do it?' You don't need anyone else to tell you where you found it difficult or where you felt that it was going well. What is important here is that you consider the role play from your own point of view. Being honest with yourself will mean that you can admit that there are areas of your performance that will benefit from further attention. At this stage you could ask yourself:

'Did I introduce myself?' – I did, but I stumbled over the words and got my role wrong. As a result I felt the bad start did not help my confidence.

'Did I listen to the role actor?' – Sometimes I found myself thinking about the next question I was going to ask rather than thinking about what was being said to me.

'Did I listen more than I talked?' – I felt that I did most of the talking without asking many questions, especially at the beginning.

'Did I stop to recap?' – I didn't really recap at all. It would have helped me, though, if I had because, at one stage, I missed some information, which afterwards was obvious.

'Did I get stuck?' – I ran out of questions after about three minutes and felt that I couldn't think of anything else to ask.

The difference between parts 1 and 2 of the process is that, at part 1, you ask yourself if you did something and, at part 2, you ask yourself how well you did it.

Having done that, you are ready for part 3, which asks 'What does this book say I should have done?' Lists of questions that may have been useful to you are listed at the end of the exercise. Think about these and ask yourself how many of them you actually used. This part of the process is designed to offer you other possibilities – other ways of dealing with the role play. It offers other perspectives and is designed to simulate the role of a personal coach. Here you are also being asked to identify the competencies being tested within the role play. Be warned, this is a suitable way to learn, but on the day of your assessment, all the time you are trying to work out which competency you are being assessed against, you are not paying full attention to what is going on in the role play. So, during the role play, just think about what is presented in front of you, and nothing more.

The last question, 4, asks 'What will I do differently in future?' You are best placed to answer this, as by now you will have thought about what happened, reflected upon how you did and read the suggested questions to identify what else you could have asked. Try to state your desired outcome in one sentence; that way it is easier to recognise. Now it is time for your Action Plan – here you identify exactly what you are going to do differently next time.

Action planning

An Action Plan is a statement of intention to arrive at a specific outcome or goal. The goal is more likely to be achieved if it is properly thought through and planned, and if the person has an active interest in achieving the goal. In other words, if you decide for yourself what you want to achieve, you will be more likely to achieve that goal than if some other person was to set the goal for you. In general, people have a tendency to procrastinate - they put off doing things in favour of other things that are more fun or involve less effort. Action planning is relatively easy. It is the 'action' that takes the effort.

An Action Plan should be SMART. That means it must be:

- **S**pecific

- **M**easurable

- **A**chievable

- **R**elevant

- **T**imed.

The Reflective Practice Sheet (see page 15) has been designed to incorporate this concept as part 5 of the process, as shown in the example below.

Desired outcome: to use more open questions

5. Action Plan	**Specific:** To use open questions during the role plays.
	Measurable: To identify the number of times closed questions are used, except when using closed questions to confirm a statement or fact.
	Achievable: This is achievable if I think about what I am doing.
	Relevant: This is relevant to the interactive exercises.
	Timed: To be completed within five days.

Advice from other people, for example your role actor, will of course be useful and that may assist you. However, they will often be talking from their own perspective and not your own. They may not recognise how you felt at the time, what you were thinking, what you were not thinking, what you found most difficult, how it was for you, etc. Only you know that, and as a result only you can decide exactly what you are going to do and how in a way that makes sense for you.

The process of reflective practice is a very personal one. The great thing about it is that it actually works. To make it work for you, you must first be honest with yourself and listen to your own advice. Remember, if you always do what you always did, you will always get what you always got.

Part 2 of this book offers role plays for you to practise. The candidate's instructions have been separated from the role actor's instructions.

As you work through this book, remember to consider the suggested questions after each exercise. By doing this you will be able to think about what you have done before rushing in, only to make the same mistakes in the same ways. It is the reflective practice that will pave the way for your own improvement. The act of reflective practice ensures that you are adequately prepared. Remember this often-used maxim: 'Fail to prepare. Prepare to fail.' Although preparation is essential, be careful not to script your interactions and learn them by heart. If you do, your interactions can become inflexible and rigid. As Helmuth Moltke, the First World War Field Marshal, observed: 'No plan survives contact' (Spiritus-temporis.com, 2008). In other words, whatever you have planned, it must be adaptable to change.

The scoring of the interactive exercises

The scoring of the interactive exercises is a complex process. What exactly are you assessed on and how are you graded? Central to the process are two areas: first, the core competencies; second, your oral communication skills.

Core competencies

For each exercise, the assessor has a checklist that lists the competencies covered in that particular exercise. You will find complete mapping of the competencies in Appendix A on page 129. Within each of those competencies the assessor is looking for certain questions and statements you are expected to make. These questions and statements are usually called 'behaviours'. For each exercise you can expect between 12 and 18 behaviours (Cox, 2007, p45). So, every time you ask a question or make a statement that is on the assessor's checklist, you score a 'positive indicator' for that behaviour. In addition, you are assessed on how well each behaviour is achieved. This is measured on a 'scalar' score. For instance, if the behaviour on the checklist is 'seek appropriate information', you can do this by asking certain questions. Some of these might be rather vague, or perhaps closed questions (e.g. 'Did something happen?'). These questions will give you a low scalar score. On the other hand, if you ask open questions, using the Magnificent Seven, you'll score higher (e.g. 'What happened?'). Link this to TED PIE and you'll score higher still (e.g. 'Tell me in detail what happened . . .'). As a general rule (Cox, 2007, p45), if you say exactly what is on the checklist you'll score a mid-point scalar. If the question or statement is more vague you'll score lower; if more thorough and in depth, you'll score higher. Behaviours and scalars are equally important: it's not just important what you do (behaviour), it's also important how you do it (scalar).

The competency Respect for Race and Diversity (RRD) is assessed throughout all the exercises: you need to consider and show respect for the opinions, circumstances and feelings of others, regardless of their race, religion, position, background, status or appearance. You need to treat everybody with dignity and respect at all times, being sensitive to individual differences.

Oral communication skills

There are two areas of oral communication the assessors focus on during the interactive exercise. First of all, they assess whether they can hear you (ranging from 'clear' to 'unclear'). It is therefore important to articulate well and make sure the volume is right. There is no need to shout, but equally don't let your nerves get in the way by whispering or mumbling! The second area is whether the assessors can understand what you say. Is your language appropriate, and is there structure and logic to your questioning and responses? You may want to avoid the use of jargon. One candidate, for instance, who previously served in the armed forces, used a lot of acronyms – common language to her. However, don't assume the assessors (or, ultimately, members of the public) are familiar with that language.

Finally, both scores (behaviour and scalar) will be taken into account when an overall score for a competency is calculated. For each competency you will be awarded an A–D grade, with A the highest. Attached to these grades are points: an A grade will give you 3 points; a B 2 points; a C 1 point; and D no points. At the end of your assessment centre day, the scores for the interactive exercise will feed into the scores for all the exercises. They will be added up and a percentage calculated, indicating whether you have passed or failed the assessment (depending on the force, the pass rate is usually 50–60 per cent).

In relation to the assessment our advice is simple. The interactive exercises are very intensive. Therefore, you will have enough to consider when role playing with the actor. The last thing you want to be thinking about is the allocation of marks, behaviours and scalars; concentrate on the exercise.

The best strategy for you to employ is just to do the very best you can.

20 tips for your interactive exercise

Before

1. Identify the contents of the core competencies.

2. As you practise, treat mistakes as learning opportunities.

3. Familiarise yourself with the contents of the Welcome Pack.

4. Keep an open mind.

5. Never assume.

6. Use notes sparingly.

7. Don't fill knowledge gaps in a whim.

8. Don't script ahead.

9. Stay in the here and now.

During

10. Listen and respond to what is being said to you.

11. If you make a mistake, move on.

12. If you are thinking it, then say it.

13. Make use of the Magnificent Seven.

14. Use open and closed questions appropriately.

15. Apply TED PIE.

16. Challenge inappropriate behaviour.

17. If you get stuck, recap.

18. Treat others as you would want to be treated yourself.

After

19. Reflect on how you have done.

20. Make an Action Plan to improve what you do.

References

Cox, P. (2007) *Passing the Police Recruit Assessment Process*. Exeter: Learning Matters.

The Interview Success Company Ltd (2009) TED PIE course handout.

National Policing Improvement Agency (2007) *Welcome Pack*. London: Home Office.

Spiritus-temporis.com (2008) Helmuth von Moltke the Elder. Available online at www.Spiritus-temporis.com/helmuth-von-moltke-the-elder/ (accessed 17 September 2008).

Further reading

Cox, P. (2007) *Passing the Police Recruit Assessment Process*. Exeter: Learning Matters.

www.theinterviewsuccesscompany.co.uk Offers guidance in relation to passing the assessment centre process and further training.

INTERACTIVE EXERCISE 1

Nat Emerson

Homophobic bullying at work

Candidate information

In this exercise there are four pages of information.

1. Memorandum from Ron Moody, Customer Service Manager, Area HQ.
2. Extract from the Staff Appraisal for Emerson from Nadine Oliver.
3. Eastshire Shopping Centre Equal Opportunities Statement.
4. Extract from Eastshire Shopping Centre Policy on Sickness.

Following the preparation period, you will be meeting Nat Emerson.

Candidate information 1.1

Memorandum

To: Customer Service Officer, Eastshire Branch
From: Customer Service Manager, Area HQ
Date: Yesterday
Subject: Sickness

Dear Colleague,

I should be grateful if you could deal with the following matter for me in my absence. Attached is a staff appraisal form concerning Nat Emerson. I have also taken the liberty of supplying you with extracts of policy pertinent to this case.

As you will note, Emerson joined the company just over six months ago and was employed as a security guard. Initially, his work was of a high standard; he was never late, his written work was acceptable and in general he appeared conscientious. However, his fine start was short-lived; his performance has declined to a standard that is no longer acceptable. Sickness appears to be the problem; he has been sick at some point every week for the last month.

Because of the high levels of absence, his colleagues are finding themselves asked to work longer hours to make up for his absence. It has now reached a level where the department is struggling to find security guards at short notice, because fewer are making themselves available.

Please feel free to deal with this matter as you think appropriate.

Ron Moody

Ron Moody

Customer Service Manager, Area HQ

Candidate information 1.2

Extract from the Staff Appraisal for Emerson

Emerson joined the company six months ago. For the first three months he appeared very highly motivated. He was smart, arrived early for work, completed his work on time and did not take any sick leave.

However, over the last three months I have noticed a dramatic fall in his performance. For example, over the last four weeks he has been sick at some time in all of those weeks. The two months preceding this he was sick every other week. Further, it is noticeable that his attitude to work has changed for the worse. For example, he appears demotivated, his written work is often left unfinished, his appearance is untidy, he is late relieving others on post and he is the first out of the door at the end of a shift.

The situation has reached a position where I feel we, the company, can no longer support such behaviour. I now request something is done about this. It is a pity for both Emerson and the company as he exhibited high potential when he first started to work here; so much so that I viewed him as an individual worthy of rapid promotion.

I feel I have no option but to forward this issue to the next level and request that this matter be formally handed to your good selves for immediate consideration.

I have attached our statement on equal opportunities because I feel his actions are not complying with this, for example 'We shall treat individuals openly and fairly with dignity and respect.' Clearly, by not supporting his work colleagues, I feel he is being disrespectful to them by being late in relieving them from their posts.

Also, you will find attached an extract of our policy on sickness.

Submitted for your attention,

Nadine Oliver

Nadine Oliver

Candidate information 1.3

Eastshire Shopping Centre Equal Opportunities Statement

Policy: 23689
Date: 17 May 2006
Topic: Equal opportunities

The Eastshire Shopping Centre seeks to employ a workforce that reflects the diversity of background and culture within which we operate, and to provide a working environment free from any form of harassment, intimidation, victimisation or unjustifiable discrimination.

We shall treat individuals openly and fairly, and with dignity and respect. We shall value their contribution towards providing a quality service to the people of Eastshire.

All members of the Eastshire Shopping Centre will demonstrate their commitment to these principles and will challenge behaviour that is unacceptable, in particular on the grounds of nationality, gender, race, colour, ethnic or national origin, disability, sexual orientation or marital status.

We shall ensure that our policies and procedures reflect these principles. This applies to all establishments within the Eastshire Shopping Centre.

Candidate information 1.4

Eastshire Shopping Centre Policy on Sickness (extract)

Policy: 6234
Date: 16 August 2005
Topic: Absence

The centre fully supports the well-being of all staff. However, staff must recognise that they have a duty to their colleagues and the public we serve to provide a certain level of service. To this end, an excessive amount of sick leave without good cause may well lead to disciplinary action.

Absence from work causes additional work to be generated for one's colleagues. If the absence is not genuine, this also has a damaging effect on morale.

Role actor's instructions 1

Nat Emerson – Homophobic bullying at work

You are Nat Emerson. You have been employed as a security guard for the last six months. The first three went really well and you were enthusiastic. Unfortunately, just after that time, you began to experience bullying at work. It started when another member of staff, Roberts, discovered that your brother is gay. Roberts had seen your brother at a function at the Hand in Spear public house with his partner. This pub is recognised by many as a gay bar. Now you find that Roberts and some of your other work colleagues are making your life difficult by mocking you in front of others at work.

You feel stuck between, on the one hand, not wanting to let your brother down, as you accept him for who and what he is without question, and, on the other hand, feeling that you want to be a part of the team. You find it increasingly difficult to deal with and the more you react to their insults, the jibes and the mocking get worse.

This has had the effect of making you not want to go to work. It has become unbearable and you feel the issue is hanging in the air all the time. As a result, it has given you sleepless nights and headaches, and because of this you have gone sick on a number of occasions. You do feel really ill, but recognise that this may be an excuse not to go into work.

Go with the role and think about how you would react to this situation yourself. Remember though that, within a role play, the acting is never too emotional either with anger or tears. Ideally the candidate will have to work to get the information from you.

A role actor will not enter into needless conversation; any talk of the weather or the football results will result in a 'yes' or 'no' and nothing further. If the candidate cannot think of anything to say, simply drop your head and stare at the floor; wait for them to sort themselves out.

Remember that the role actor will normally have a maximum of about 20 lines, so try to keep to that. This means that you will have to be prepared to improvise as you go, without changing the emphasis of the exercise.

When the candidate enters, say:

'I am Nat Emerson; I understand you want to see me.'

If asked for the reason as to why you are taking so much sickness, say:

'I am unable to sleep and have headaches.'

If you are asked if you have sought medical attention, say:

'No, I haven't.'

If asked the reason for this, say:

'I don't think it is something I can get medication for.'

If asked what is wrong or if you need help, say:

'There is nothing you can do, I think.'

If asked the reason why, explain the account about your brother and the effect the taunting is having on you.

If asked who is responsible, state that it is mostly Roberts and make up some other names, both male and female.

Following your account, say:

'I just feel that I can't come to work any more. Just the thought of it makes me sick. I've had enough.'

If the candidate suggests a certain course of action, say:

'Yes, if you think that's best.'

Suggested candidate questions and responses

Role actor: 'I am unable to sleep and have headaches.'

Your possible responses:

- Is there a reason for this?
- Please tell me in detail about your inability to sleep.
- Please tell me in detail about your headaches.

Role actor: 'No, I haven't' (*sought medical attention*).

- Is there a reason for not doing so?
- Please explain to me exactly why you have not sought medical attention.

Role actor: 'I don't think it is something I can get medication for.'

- Why is that?
- Why would you not be able to get medication?
- What is it about your condition that medication would not help?

Role actor: 'There is nothing you can do, I think.'

- Why is that?
- Please explain to me precisely why that is.
- Please tell me exactly why you think that.

After hearing about the account of Nat's brother and the effect the taunting is having on him . . .

- The Eastshire Shopping Centre does not tolerate bullying and neither do I. The behaviour of your colleagues will not be tolerated. I will take personal responsibility for dealing with this issue.

Role actor: 'I just feel that I can't come to work any more. Just the thought of it makes me sick. I've had enough.'

- I can assure you that I will do all I can to make your situation here more tolerable.

- I propose that we consider your needs in detail and discuss how we can accommodate you.

- What I believe is needed is for those involved with this bullying to be suspended from duty following my investigation. Following this, I will consider with whom you will prefer to work.

- You are welcome to a course of counselling from a professional body; of course, this will be at the expense of the company. I will see to it personally that this is done.

Task

In relation to the competencies, list those you consider have been tested in this interactive exercise. The answers are given at the end of this book.

INTERACTIVE EXERCISE 2

Jo Chi

Gay bar

Candidate information

In this exercise there are three pages of information.

1. Memorandum from Ron Moody, Customer Service Manager, Area HQ.
2. Eastshire Shopping Centre Equal Opportunities Statement.
3. Letter of complaint from Jo Chi.

Following the preparation period, you will be meeting Jo Chi.

Candidate information 2.1

Memorandum

To: Customer Service Officer, Eastshire Branch
From: Customer Service Manager, Area HQ
Date: Yesterday
Subject: The behaviour of patrons within the Spear in Hand public house

Dear Colleague,

I have received a letter of complaint from Jo Chi. Apparently, he is upset at some of the behaviour in the Spear in Hand public house. It would appear that he is not aware that the bar is renowned as a gay bar.

He will be attending to see you today to complain about two men he witnessed kissing in the bar area. I know I can rely on you to handle this sensitively. For your information I have attached a copy of our statement on equal opportunities just to ensure you are fully up to date.

Ron Moody

Ron Moody

Customer Service Manager, Area HQ

Candidate information 2.2

Eastshire Shopping Centre Equal Opportunities Statement

Policy: 23689
Date: 17 May 2005
Topic: Equal opportunities

The Eastshire Shopping Centre seeks to employ a workforce that reflects the diversity of background and culture within which we operate, and to provide a working environment free from any form of harassment, intimidation, victimisation or unjustifiable discrimination.

We shall treat individuals openly and fairly, and with dignity and respect. We shall value their contribution towards providing a quality service to the people of Eastshire.

All members of the Eastshire Shopping Centre will demonstrate their commitment to these principles and will challenge behaviour that is unacceptable, in particular on the grounds of nationality, gender, race, colour, ethnic or national origin, disability, sexual orientation or marital status.

We shall ensure that our policies and procedures reflect these principles. This applies to all establishments within the Eastshire Shopping Centre.

Candidate information 2.3

Letter of complaint from Jo Chi

Dear Mr Moody,

I am writing to you to complain about the appalling behaviour witnessed by myself within the Spear in Hand public house. Yesterday evening, my mother and myself attended the aforementioned public house for refreshment. We saw what can only be described as outrageous behaviour by some of the other gentlemen in the bar area.

My mother and I saw two gentlemen holding hands and hugging each other inappropriately. Then they began to kiss each other. I don't mean a peck on the cheek; this was a full-on French kiss. I was almost sick into my drink. To think that such behaviour can carry on in public is beyond me. My mother, who is 82, was appalled. I asked them to stop and they ignored my request, so I complained to the barman. He just laughed in my face. We left our drinks and will never be going back.

Such behaviour cannot be tolerated in today's society. I demand that something be done!

Yours sincerely,

Jo Chi

Jo Chi

Role actor's instructions 2

Jo Chi – Gay bar

You are Jo Chi, a member of the public. You have been invited to the meeting to discuss the issue you have raised in relation to men kissing in the bar area of the Spear in Hand public house. You were in company with your mother and you both saw two gentlemen holding hands and hugging each other. You believed this to be inappropriate. You then noticed that they had begun to kiss each other with what you described as a full-on French kiss. You were almost sick into your drink. To think that such behaviour can carry on in public is beyond you. Your mother, who is 82, was appalled.

You asked them to stop and they ignored your request, so you complained to the barman. He just laughed in your face. You both left your drinks and intend never going back. You are outwardly anti-gay (homophobic).

Go with the role and think about how you would react to this situation yourself. Remember though that, within a role play, the acting is never too emotional either with anger or tears. Ideally, the candidate will have to work to get the information from you.

A role actor will not enter into needless conversation; any talk of the weather or the football results will result in a 'yes' or 'no' and nothing further. If the candidate cannot think of anything to say, simply drop your head and stare at the floor; wait for them to sort themselves out.

Remember that the role actor will normally have a maximum of about 20 lines, so try to keep to this. This means that you will have to be prepared to improvise as you go, without changing the emphasis of the exercise.

When the candidate enters, say:

'I am Jo Chi; I'm here about the outrageous behaviour in the pub.'

At an appropriate time, say:

'The behaviour is just not natural.'

If pursued, say:

'I don't think that the queens should be allowed out in public.'

If you are challenged, accept the challenge; otherwise say:

'You have your views and I have mine, but man on man sex I cannot condone.'

You are unwilling to accept that such behaviour should be tolerated and feel that everyone has been unwilling to see things from your point of view.

At an appropriate place, say:

'I feel that you are being unsympathetic to both my mother and myself; why are you not willing to sort this out?'

If you are asked what you would like to be done, say:

'Close the pub!'

Suggested candidate questions and responses

Role actor: 'I am Jo Chi; I'm here about the outrageous behaviour in the pub.'

Your possible responses:

- Please describe to me exactly what happened in the public house that day.

- I have read your letter; please tell me in detail what happened while you were in the pub.

Role actor: 'The behaviour is just not natural.'

- You refer to the behaviour being not natural. What do you mean exactly?

- I don't know if you are aware, but this pub has a reputation for being a gay bar, so it is not uncommon for people of the same sex to behave in the way you describe.

Role actor: 'I don't think that the queens should be allowed out in public.'

- Let me stop you there. It is wholly inappropriate for you to use the word 'queens' in this way. The words 'gay' or 'homosexual' are appropriate terms.

- I challenge that comment; it is offensive to gay people and I don't like it.

Role actor: 'You have your views and I have mine, but man on man sex I cannot condone.'

- That is a matter for you and you alone.

- That is a matter for you, but on this occasion you were in a gay bar where gay people felt able to express themselves in this way. I feel in this instance you have no cause for complaint.

Role actor: 'I feel that you are being unsympathetic to both my mother and myself; why are you not willing to sort this out?'

- I am sorry you feel this way about this situation; I think that an alternative public house would be appropriate for you and your mother.

- I can see that you not realising that the pub is frequented by gay people can cause a problem.

- I will meet with the owners of the pub and discuss if it would be appropriate to place a notice at the entrance.

  If you asked what the role actor would like to be done, the reply would be: 'Close the pub!'

- That is out of the question.

- Is there anything further I can assist you with today?

Task
In relation to the competencies, list those you consider have been tested in this interactive exercise. The answers are given at the end of this book.

INTERACTIVE EXERCISE 3

Muhtarem Mustafa

Halal shop

Candidate information

In this exercise there are three pages of information.

1. Memorandum from Ron Moody, Customer Service Manager, Area HQ.
2. Letter from Muhtarem Mustafa.
3. Eastshire Shopping Centre Equal Opportunities Statement.

Following the preparation period, you will be meeting Muhtarem Mustafa.

Candidate information 3.1

Memorandum

To: Customer Service Officer, Eastshire Branch
From: Customer Service Manager, Area HQ
Date: Yesterday
Subject: Racism at the Halal shop

Dear Colleague,

I have received a letter of concern in relation to the situation at the Halal shop. They are experiencing trouble from what they believe to be a group of youths; nothing too bad at the moment but I am worried that this could escalate. I first heard about this last Saturday when I attended the Shop Watch meeting. I requested the owner of the shop, Muhtarem Mustafa, to record the staff's concerns in a formal letter as the basis for us to start our investigation. There is no need to contact the police at this time as I believe that positive action on our part will prevent an escalation of the situation. Muhtarem Mustafa has been invited by me personally to see you today. Please deal with this matter as you see fit.

Ron Moody

Ron Moody

Customer Service Manager, Area HQ

Candidate information 3.2

Letter from Muhtarem Mustafa

Dear Mr Moody,

I did not want to bother you, but having spoken about this it seems that I should write to explain about the youths I told you about. They come to the shop and ask for bacon bites and pork scratchings. It seems a fun thing for them, but it is not so much fun for us. I see the other boys outside waiting and laughing. This is not good for custom and it is now bothering the people in the shop. They are not concerned by the talk of pork, but of the fact that the youths are seeing us as people to laugh at and to taunt. It is time I think now to stop it and to have them spoken to. It is the same group time and time again.

Yours sincerely,

Muhtarem Mustafa

Muhtarem Mustafa

Candidate information 3.3

Eastshire Shopping Centre Equal Opportunities Statement

Policy: 23689
Date: 17 May 2006
Topic: Equal opportunities

The Eastshire Shopping Centre seeks to employ a workforce that reflects the diversity of background and culture within which we operate, and to provide a working environment free from any form of harassment, intimidation, victimisation or unjustifiable discrimination.

We shall treat individuals openly and fairly, and with dignity and respect. We shall value their contribution towards providing a quality service to the people of Eastshire.

All members of the Eastshire Shopping Centre will demonstrate their commitment to these principles and will challenge behaviour that is unacceptable, in particular on the grounds of nationality, gender, race, colour, ethnic or national origin, disability, sexual orientation or marital status.

We shall ensure that our policies and procedures reflect these principles. This applies to all establishments within the Eastshire Shopping Centre.

Role actor's instructions 3

Muhtarem Mustafa – Halal shop

You are Muhtarem Mustafa, the owner of the Halal Meat Shop in Eastshire Shopping Centre. You have been having some problems recently with some youths. They come to the shop and ask for bacon bites and pork scratchings. It seems a bit like a dare for them and a fun thing for them to be doing, but it is not so much fun for you. You see the other boys outside the shop waiting and laughing. You feel that this is not good for custom and it is now bothering the people in the shop. They are not concerned by the talk of pork, but just the fact that the youths are seeing you as people to laugh at and to taunt. You feel that it is time now to stop this behaviour and to have them spoken to. It is the same group on each occasion.

What you know and the candidate does not is that these boys are of school age and, during the time of most incidents, they should be attending school.

Go with the role and think about how you would react to this situation yourself. Remember though that, within a role play, the acting is never too emotional either with anger or tears. Ideally, the candidate will have to work to get the information from you.

A role actor will not enter into needless conversation; any talk of the weather or the football results will result in a 'yes' or 'no' and nothing further. If the candidate cannot think of anything to say, simply drop your head and stare at the floor; wait for them to sort themselves out.

Remember that the role actor will normally have a maximum of about 20 lines, so try to keep to that. This means that you will have to be prepared to improvise as you go, without changing the emphasis of the exercise.

When the candidate enters, say:

'I am Muhtarem Mustafa. I am here to see you about the behaviour of the boys in my shop.'

When questioned about this, say:

'One comes in and asks for bacon bites or pork scratchings and the others wait outside and laugh.'

If asked about the effect of this, say:

'The customers are getting fed up with the taunting; it is bad for custom.'

At an appropriate stage, say:

'I would expect more from these children.'

If picked up on, explain that you recognise the school uniform (make it up and describe it) and you know they should be at school.

If not picked up on, ask:

'What is the school doing about it?'

If the candidate suggests a course of action, say:

'Oh well, if you think that is best.'

Suggested candidate questions and responses

Role actor: 'I am Muhtarem Mustafa. I am here to see you about the behaviour of the boys in my shop.'

Your possible responses.

- Thank you for coming to see me today. How can I help you in relation to these boys?
- Please tell me in detail what the situation is with the boys.
- Do you know these boys?

Role actor: 'One comes in and asks for bacon bites or pork scratchings and the others wait outside and laugh.'

- How often has this happened?
- How many of them are there?
- Is it the same group every time?
- Tell me exactly what they say to you.
- What effect is this having upon your custom?

Role actor: 'The customers are getting fed up with the taunting; it is bad for custom.'

- Yes, I can see how this can be irritating.
- Please describe to me exactly how they taunt you.

Role actor: 'I would expect more from these children.'

- Why is that?
- What is it about these children that makes you think you would expect more from them?

If this was picked up on, the role actor was instructed to explain that they recognise the school uniform and they know the children should be at school.

If not picked up on, the role actor would ask: 'What is the school doing about it?'

- What do you mean exactly?
- Please describe to me precisely what interest the school has in these children.
- Are these children in school uniform?
- Do you recognise that uniform?

It will be appropriate for you to make a proposal, e.g.:

I will take personal responsibility for assisting you with this matter. I will:

- ensure that CCTV is monitoring your establishment;
- identify the children involved;
- contact the school;
- contact the local authority in relation to non-attendance;
- contact the children's parents;
- ensure that there is a visible presence of security guards in the vicinity of your shop.

Task

In relation to the competencies, list those you consider have been tested in this interactive exercise. The answers are given at the end of this book.

INTERACTIVE EXERCISE 4

Peta/Peter Godley

Rats in the restaurant

Candidate information

In this exercise there are three pages of information.

1. Memorandum from Ron Moody, Customer Service Manager, Area HQ.
2. Report from Gary Star, Executive Officer, Health and Safety.
3. Letter of complaint from Lee Rose.

Following the preparation period, you will be meeting Peta/Peter Godley.

Candidate information 4.1

Memorandum

To: Customer Service Officer, Eastshire Branch
From: Customer Service Manager, Area HQ
Date: Yesterday
Subject: Rats at the Banshees restaurant

Dear Colleague,

I have received a letter of complaint from various members of the public and local businesses in relation to the existence of rats behind the Banshees restaurant. This has been investigated and a report is attached. It appears that there are rats inhabiting the rear of the restaurant, but the exact location has not been established.

Peta/Peter Godley, the restaurant owner, will be attending today to discuss the matter with you. Please deal with this as you feel appropriate.

Ron Moody

Ron Moody

Customer Service Manager, Area HQ

Candidate information 4.2

Report

Investigation into allegation of the presence of rats at the Banshees restaurant

Gary Star – Executive Officer, Health and Safety

Following a number of complaints from various business owners and members of the public in relation to the sightings of rats in the vicinity of the Banshees restaurant, I have been tasked with assessing the situation. I attended the location and noticed that, in general, the immediate area was clean and devoid of rubbish. However, closer examination of the area immediately behind the Banshees restaurant revealed an excess of rubbish. The bins appeared full and, as a consequence, rubbish was being piled up on the floor. The rubbish consists of waste food, cans, bottles, food wrappings, etc.

During my visit, the restaurant was closed and so I was unable to inspect the interior of the establishment or speak to the staff.

Further inspection revealed the presence of rats' droppings, but I was unable to identify the exact location of the nest. I left the premises and watched from inside my car. After only three or four minutes I saw a total of three rats enter the rear of the premises.

There is a Health and Safety issue here that I recommend should be dealt with immediately.

Candidate information 4.3

Letter of complaint from Lee Rose

Dear Mr Moody,

I am writing to inform you about a problem with the Banshees restaurant next door in relation to rats.

We have noticed the existence of the rats for quite a while now and the situation seems to be getting worse. As a result, I spoke to the owner. Unfortunately, they denied all knowledge and suggested I was making malicious allegations against them; this was not true.

In light of this, we feel that we have no option but to make an official complaint to you and we ask that something be done soon. We have seen the rats walk over our bottles and can't risk an outbreak of Weil's disease.

We trust you can resolve this matter to our satisfaction.

Yours sincerely,

LEE ROSE

Lee Rose

Spear in Hand public house

Role actor's instructions 4

Peta/Peter Godley – Rats in the restaurant

You are Peta/Peter Godley, the owner of the Banshees restaurant. You have been invited to the meeting to discuss the issue of the existence of vermin at the rear of your restaurant.

Go with the role and think about how you would react to this situation yourself. Remember though that, within a role play, the acting is never too emotional either with anger or tears. Ideally, the candidate will have to work to get the information from you.

A role actor will not enter into needless conversation; any talk of the weather or the football results will result in a 'yes' or 'no' and nothing further. If the candidate cannot think of anything to say, simply drop your head and stare at the floor; wait for them to sort themselves out.

Remember that the role actor will normally have a maximum of about 20 lines, so try to keep to this. This means that you will have to be prepared to improvise as you go, without changing the emphasis of the exercise.

What you know and the candidate does not is the extent of the problem. You know that rats have infested the fast-food shop next door to you.

When the candidate enters, say:

'I am Peta/Peter Godley; I understand you want to speak to me.'

At first deny there is a problem and say:

'I don't know what you are talking about; there is no problem with rats.'

Later, agree that they may exist but say you have never seen one.

If asked what you are going to do about it, say:

'The cause of the problem is not my doing.'

If asked why, explain that the 'powers that be' at the shopping centre decided on the introduction of a two-week collection system. The first week is for recyclable goods and the second for normal rubbish. As a consequence, you find yourself knee-deep in rubbish. (If this is not picked up on, repeat the line above.)

If asked, you have four bins of recyclable rubbish and four bins of normal rubbish.

At an appropriate stage, say:

'What are you going to do about the rats?'

At an appropriate time, say:

'You are making out the problem is mine; it's the system that is at fault and that's your responsibility.'

At an appropriate time, say:

'What are you going to do about the rats coming from the fast-food shop next door?'

You have seen many rats eating leftover food in the dustbins and feel that they have spread to your establishment – make up the details as you think fit.

Suggested candidate questions and responses

Role actor: 'I don't know what you are talking about, there is no problem with rats.'

Your possible responses.

- It has been drawn to my attention that there may be a problem with rats at the rear of your premises.
- (*Refer to the Executive Officer, Health and Safety report.*) I am not here to judge you, just to assist you with this matter, if you will permit me.
- (*Refer to the Executive Officer, Health and Safety report.*) It appears there may be a problem according to this expert. Perhaps we can discuss the way forward.
- I would like you to appreciate that I am here to help you, not prosecute you.

The role actor later agrees that the rats may exist, but that he or she has never seen one.

- Yes, rats can be quite bright, I understand, and are quick to hide when someone approaches.
- I am not surprised; they have a reputation for keeping out of sight.
- Not seeing one does not mean that the problem does not exist. What do you think you can do about this situation?

If you asked what they are going to do about it, the reply was:

'The cause of the problem is not my doing.'

- Why do you say that?
- What do you mean?
- Why is it not your doing?
- Please explain to me why you believe this is not your doing.

You were told that the 'powers that be' at the shopping centre decided on the introduction of a bi-weekly collection – the first week for recyclable goods and the second for normal rubbish. As a consequence, the role actor is knee-deep in rubbish.

- Obviously this system is not working; I propose we have weekly collections.
- How many bins do you have at present?
- Perhaps it would be appropriate to invest in more bins?
- How many bins do you require?
- What do you propose may help solve the problem?

Role actor: 'What are you going to do about the rats?'

- We will offer you all the assistance we can. What is required is for the Health and Safety expert to be given access to the inside of the building in order to identify the problem fully.

- We can arrange for the bins to be emptied more regularly; we will send a report to the Eastshire local authority.

- We will pay for half of the new bins you require.

- We will meet the cost of all the bins you require.

Role actor: 'You are making out the problem is mine; it's the system that is at fault and that's your responsibility.'

- I feel this is a shared problem and, as such, feel that co-operation between us will be beneficial.

- Please explain to me in detail exactly what you would like to have happen.

Role actor: 'What are you going to do about the rats coming from the fast-food shop next door?'

- What can you tell me about this?

- Describe to me in detail the situation next door.

- Do you know of any other establishments infested with rats?

- Is there anything further you would like to discuss?

- Is there any other matter with which you feel I can assist you?

Task

In relation to the competencies, list those you consider have been tested in this interactive exercise. The answers are given at the end of this book.

INTERACTIVE EXERCISE 5

Rennie Chandler

Assistance refused

Candidate information

In this exercise there are three pages of information.

1. Memorandum from Ron Moody, Customer Service Manager, Area HQ.
2. Eastshire Shopping Centre Equal Opportunities Statement.
3. Letter of complaint from Rennie Chandler.

Following the preparation period, you will be meeting Rennie Chandler.

Candidate information 5.1

Memorandum

To: Customer Service Officer, Eastshire Branch
From: Customer Service Manager, Area HQ
Date: Yesterday
Subject: Assistance to disabled person refused

Dear Colleague,

Please see the attached letter of complaint from Rennie Chandler. I have included our Equal Opportunities Statement, as it is the only document I can find that may cover this problem.

If this is not handled in the correct manner, we could be facing huge problems! Please deal with this as you think appropriate.

Ron Moody

Ron Moody

Customer Service Manager, Area HQ

Candidate information 5.2

Eastshire Shopping Centre Equal Opportunities Statement

Policy: 23689
Date: 17 May 2006
Topic: Equal opportunities

The Eastshire Shopping Centre seeks to employ a workforce that reflects the diversity of background and culture within which we operate, and to provide a working environment free from any form of harassment, intimidation, victimisation or unjustifiable discrimination.

We shall treat individuals openly and fairly, and with dignity and respect. We shall value their contribution towards providing a quality service to the people of Eastshire.

All members of the Eastshire Shopping Centre will demonstrate their commitment to these principles and will challenge behaviour that is unacceptable, in particular on the grounds of nationality, gender, race, colour, ethnic or national origin, disability, sexual orientation or marital status.

We shall ensure that our policies and procedures reflect these principles. This applies to all establishments within the Eastshire Shopping Centre.

Candidate information 5.3

Letter of complaint from Rennie Chandler

To the Manager of Security,

I am a wheelchair user and regular shopper at the centre. Last week, I discovered that my usual route from the disabled car bay to the shopping centre was obstructed by some building works.

The effect of this was that I encountered difficulty negotiating the stairs to the shopping centre, as the ramp I usually used was covered in scaffolding. However, I obtained help from a member of the public who took me up the stairs.

On my way back, anticipating a similar problem getting back down, I saw a security guard and asked them for assistance. They replied that, for health and safety reasons, they were not able to help me as my weight might damage their back.

I knew about a lift that was used for moving goods and asked the security guard if they would assist me by escorting me to the lift. I was told that the lift was out of order.

I cannot believe that I have been treated in this way. I will be available to discuss this matter any time next week.

Yours sincerely,

Rennie Chandler

Rennie Chandler

Role actor's instructions 5

Rennie Chandler – Assistance refused

You are Rennie Chandler, a wheelchair user and regular shopper at the Eastshire Shopping Centre. Last week, you discovered that your usual route from the disabled car bay to the shopping centre was obstructed by some building works. The effect of this was that you encountered difficulty negotiating the stairs to the shopping centre as the ramp you usually used was covered in scaffolding. Undaunted, you obtained help from a member of the public who took you up the stairs.

On your way back, anticipating a similar problem getting back down, you saw a security guard and asked them for assistance. They replied that, for health and safety reasons, they were not able to help you as your weight might damage their back. You knew about a lift that was used for moving goods and asked the security guard if they would assist you by escorting you to the lift. You were told that the lift was out of order at that time. You recognise the guard's accent as Eastern European.

What you know but the candidate does not is that you made your way to the lift (entering a restricted area not open to the public) and found the lift to be working. Your enquiries revealed that the lift had not been broken recently. You are here to complain. You are less than happy.

Go with the role and think about how you would react to this situation yourself. Remember though that, within a role play, the acting is never too emotional either with anger or tears. Ideally the candidate will have to work to get the information from you.

A role actor will not enter into needless conversation; any talk of the weather or the football results will result in a 'yes' or 'no' and nothing further. If the candidate cannot think of anything to say, simply drop your head and stare at the floor; wait for them to sort themselves out.

Remember that the role actor will normally have a maximum of about 20 lines, so try to keep to this. This means that you will have to be prepared to improvise as you go, without changing the emphasis of the exercise.

When the candidate enter, say:

> 'I am Rennie Chandler; I am here to see you about the way in which I have been treated.'

State the situation above but do not mention the lift yet. Demand for the security guard to be dealt with, stating:

> 'Is this how your security guards are trained to help those in need?'

At an appropriate time, say:

> 'Why employ Eastern Europeans anyway? They are nothing but trouble.'

If you are not challenged at this point, say:

'You see, they are just lazy thieves; the only reason we had the Berlin wall built was to keep them out.' (Please change the nationality if necessary so as not to cause offence.)

You do not have a name of the security guard as, from where you were sitting, you could not read the name on their badge.

It is the attitude that has really made you angry. If asked what you want done, say:

'For the security guard to see the error of their ways.'

At an appropriate time, say:

'What really made me cross was the lie.'

If picked up on, say:

'The other goods lift was working, I checked it; I was lied to.'

If this is not picked up on, say:

'Your security guard lied to me! The other goods lift was working, I checked it; this is totally unacceptable!

If the candidate suggests a certain course of action, say:

'Yes, if you think that's best.'

Suggested candidate questions and responses

The role actor will give an account of the situation and will demand for the security guard to be dealt with.

Your possible responses.

- I am sorry to hear that you have been treated in this way; please accept my unreserved apologies. I will ensure that this never happens again.

- To ensure that I have all the details necessary for me to investigate this matter fully, please tell me in detail what occurred.

- In order to deal with the security guard, I require a detailed description of the individual. Please describe to me in detail what the security guard looked like.

Role actor: 'Is this how your security guards are trained to help those in need?'

- I feel that, on this occasion, you have been treated very badly and I would like to apologise to you for the hurt you may have felt. The security guards should be aware of our policy in relation to matters of equality. (*Refer to the Equal Opportunities Statement*.)

- I think you have made a good point. It is painfully obvious to me that, in this instance, a security guard was lacking in either the knowledge of our equal opportunities policy or was unwilling to fulfil their obligations. Please accept my apologies.

Role actor: 'Why employ Eastern Europeans anyway? They are nothing but trouble.'

- Let me stop you there. I challenge your assertion that all Eastern Europeans are nothing but trouble. Please do not generalise in this way.

If you did not challenge this statement, you would have been given another opportunity to challenge here:

Role actor: 'You see they are just lazy thieves; the only reason we had the Berlin Wall built was to keep them out.'

- What you say is highly inappropriate and I find it offensive. Please do not refer to Eastern Europeans as thieves. I feel your theory about the Berlin Wall should be kept to yourself. I suggest we continue this conversation in an adult manner and not reduce the conversation to name calling.

Having challenged the inappropriate behaviour, it would be appropriate to ask for the name of the security guard or to take a description.

If you had asked what Rennie wanted done, you would have heard: 'For the security guard to see the error of his ways.'

- I propose identifying the individual concerned to ascertain why they did not assist you or ask for assistance to help you.

- Following this, I will ensure that all staff are fully appraised of our equal opportunities policies.

Role actor: 'What really made me cross was the lie.'

- What do you mean?

- Please tell me in detail what you mean.

- Please tell me precisely how you have been lied to.

Role actor: 'The other goods lift was working, I checked it; I was lied to.' Or: 'Your security guard lied to me! The other goods lift was working, I checked it; this is totally unacceptable!'

- I am very sorry to hear that you have been lied to; there is no excuse for this. I am considering dealing with this as a disciplinary matter because this is simply not on.

- Please accept my apologies. I will ensure that this matter is dealt with personally.

- I feel that you have been treated very poorly indeed. I would invite you to take my telephone number and, whenever you attend this centre, please ring me and I will see to it that you are afforded all the assistance you require.

- How else can I assist you?

- Are there any other matters that you would like to draw to my attention?

Task

In relation to the competencies, list those you consider have been tested in this interactive exercise. The answers are given at the end of this book.

INTERACTIVE EXERCISE 6

Jordan Rose

Bad language

Candidate information

In this exercise there are three pages of information.

1. Memorandum from Ron Moody, Customer Service Manager, Area HQ.
2. Eastshire Shopping Centre Equal Opportunities Statement.
3. Letter of complaint from Gordon Cooper.

Following the preparation period, you will be meeting Jordan Rose.

Candidate information 6.1

Memorandum

To: Customer Service Officer, Eastshire Branch
From: Customer Service Manager, Area HQ
Date: Yesterday
Subject: Bad language in the Spear in Hand public house

Dear Colleague,

I have received a letter from Gordon Cooper complaining about the use of bad language within the Spear in Hand public house in the Eastshire Shopping Centre. The individual appears quite concerned that it is interfering with his comfort while having a quiet drink with his wife. The letter of complaint is attached. I have also attached the Eastshire Shopping Centre Equal Opportunities Statement for your information. This is not the first time I have received a complaint about the behaviour of some patrons within this pub. I have located Jordan Rose, the barperson and part owner of the pub, who has agreed to attend to see you today. Please deal with this in any way you think fit.

Ron Moody

Ron Moody

Customer Service Manager, Area HQ

Candidate information 6.2

Eastshire Shopping Centre Equal Opportunities Statement

Policy: 23689
Date: 17 May 2006
Topic: Equal opportunities

The Eastshire Shopping Centre seeks to employ a workforce that reflects the diversity of background and culture within which we operate, and to provide a working environment free from any form of harassment, intimidation, victimisation or unjustifiable discrimination.

We shall treat individuals openly and fairly, and with dignity and respect. We shall value their contribution towards providing a quality service to the people of Eastshire.

All members of the Eastshire Shopping Centre will demonstrate their commitment to these principles and will challenge behaviour that is unacceptable, in particular on the grounds of nationality, gender, race, colour, ethnic or national origin, disability, sexual orientation or marital status.

We shall ensure that our policies and procedures reflect these principles. This applies to all establishments within the Eastshire Shopping Centre.

Candidate information 6.3

Letter of complaint from Gordon Cooper

Dear Sir,

I am writing to you to in respect of the bad language that some patrons are using in the Spear in Hand public house within the Eastshire Shopping Centre. I have been a resident of Eastshire for over 22 years and recently I have found that my comfort is being impaired by the use of loud music in a number of shops and restaurants. I cannot hear myself think or make myself heard over the sound of the music. As a result, my wife and I have frequented this particular public house because they have no music playing during the day. However, recently I have experienced some very bad language used by the customers. I am a man of the world, but I feel that the use of the C-word, F-word and MF-word is not appropriate. My wife was quite put out by the language; as a result we left our drinks and headed for home.

I do not feel that I have to put up with this kind of language. Furthermore, the barperson, Jordan, did nothing to stop what was going on and they were actually sitting at the bar! Please do something.

Yours faithfully,

Gordon Cooper

Gordon Cooper

Role actor's instructions 6

Jordan Rose – Bad language

You are Jordan Rose. You are the barperson and part owner of the Spear in Hand public house, Eastshire Shopping Centre.

The reason you have been invited in today is that there have been a number of complaints regarding the use of bad language in your pub. One such complaint has come from a Mr Gordon Cooper, who has said that, recently, he has experienced some very bad language used by the customers. He has complained about the use of the C-, F- and MF-words, which he considers are not appropriate. He and his wife were quite put out by the language, so they left their drinks and headed for home. Gordon does not feel that he has to put up with this kind of language. Furthermore, he is alleging that you, Jordan, the barperson, did nothing to stop what was going on and that those responsible were actually sitting at the bar!

Go with the role and think about how you would react to this situation yourself. Remember though that, within a role play, the acting is never too emotional either with anger or tears. Ideally, the candidate will have to work to get the information from you.

A role actor will not enter into needless conversation; any talk of the weather or the football results will result in a 'yes' or 'no' and nothing further. If the candidate cannot think of anything to say, simply drop your head and stare at the floor; wait for them to sort themselves out.

Remember that the role actor will normally have a maximum of about 20 lines, so try to keep to this. This means that you will have to be prepared to improvise as you go, without changing the emphasis of the exercise.

What you know and the candidate does not is that those responsible for the bad language are off-duty security guards who work in the Eastshire Shopping Centre. They have finished their shift and regularly let off a bit of steam. You don't know all of their names, but you heard the name Nat mentioned.

When the candidate enters, say:

'I am Jordan Rose and am here to see you about the language problem in the pub.'

If asked about the use of the bad language, say:

'Yes, I agree it is not acceptable.'

If asked what you heard them say, say:

'The F- and C-words.'

If asked what you are going to do about it, say:

'I find it rather difficult to challenge these people.'

If asked why, say:

'I don't know if I'm up to it really.'

If asked why, say:

'Well, it's never easy with this group.'

If asked why or what you mean, say:

'Well, they are security guards from the Eastshire Shopping Centre. I know they should not do it, but it's a bit embarrassing really, because sometimes I need their assistance.'

If this line of enquiry is not pursued, then say at an appropriate stage:

'You know it's surprising that they can do this; I would have expected more from them really.'

If this is picked up on, say:

'Well, they are security guards from the Eastshire Shopping Centre. I know they should not do it, but it's a bit embarrassing really, because sometimes I need their assistance.'

If asked who they are, say:

'I only heard one name and that was Nat.'

If asked for a description, state they were in the usual black trousers and white shirts, but with no epaulettes, and they were wearing black boots. Make the rest up.

If the candidate suggests a certain course of action, say:

'Yes, if you think that's best.'

Suggested candidate questions and responses

Role actor: 'Yes, I agree it is not acceptable.'

Your possible responses:

- Did you hear what they were saying exactly?
- What did you hear them saying exactly?

Role actor: 'The F- and C-words.'

- Was that the extent of the bad language?
- Did you hear any other bad language?
- What was the reaction of the other patrons?

Role actor: 'I find it rather difficult to challenge these people.'

- Explain to me exactly why you find this difficult.
- Explain to me precisely why this is difficult.

Role actor: 'I don't know if I'm up to it really.'

- In what way exactly?
- Tell me exactly why you are not up to it.

Role actor: 'Well, it's never easy with this group.'

- What is it about this group that is not easy?
- Explain to me precisely what is not easy with this group.

Role actor: 'Well, they are security guards from the Eastshire Shopping Centre. I know they should not do it, but it's a bit embarrassing really, because sometimes I need their assistance.'

- Let me first apologise for their unacceptable behaviour. I want you to appreciate that we consider such behaviour to be totally unacceptable. I will take personal responsibility to ensure that these people are identified and dealt with appropriately.

Having dealt with the apology, etc., possible responses are:

- Please tell me exactly who these security guards are.
- Please describe to me in detail the security guards using the bad language.

(The following will be used if they have not been identified as security guards above.)

Role actor: 'You know, it is surprising that they can do this. I would have expected more from them really.'

- Why would you have expected more from these people?
- What is it about this group of people that you would have expected more from?

Role actor: 'I only heard one name and that was Nat.'

- Did you hear any other names used?
- Please describe in detail Nat's appearance.
- Please describe the group in detail.
- Are there any specific features about this group?

Task
In relation to the competencies, list those you consider have been tested in this interactive exercise. The answers are given at the end of this book.

INTERACTIVE EXERCISE 7

Sandi Smith

Beggars

Candidate information

In this exercise there are four pages of information.

1. Memorandum from Ron Moody, Customer Service Manager, Area HQ.
2. Letter of complaint from Sandi Smith.
3. Eastshire Shopping Centre Policy on Begging.
4. Eastshire Shopping Centre Policy on Smoking.

Following the preparation period, you will be meeting Sandi Smith.

Candidate information 7.1

Memorandum

To: Customer Service Officer, Eastshire Branch
From: Customer Service Manager, Area HQ
Date: Yesterday
Subject: Beggars

Dear Colleague,

I would like you to deal with the following complaint. Please see the attached letter from Sandi Smith. It appears simple enough, so I'm sure you will be able to deal with this with no problem. I have attached all that I can find on the subject to assist you.

Sandi has been invited to see you today.

Ron Moody

Ron Moody

Customer Service Manager, Area HQ

Candidate information 7.2

Letter of complaint from Sandi Smith

Dear Sir,

I wish to complain in the strongest possible terms about the beggars that frequent the entrance to the shopping centre.

I find it intolerable that I am forced to put up with begging every time I enter the centre. I am asked for money and am made to feel guilty when I choose not to give. Your customers should not have to put up with this.

I notice they have the money to smoke!

There are two of them, one male and one female. They sit at either side of the large corridor at the entrance to the centre and are an obstruction.

Please do something about this immediately!

Yours faithfully,

Sandi Smith

Sandi Smith

Candidate information 7.3

Eastshire Shopping Centre Policy on Begging

Policy: 18489
Date: 16 August 2004
Topic: Begging

Scope

Begging for money, goods or acts of kindness.

Purpose

To prevent individuals begging.

Action

No individual will be *permitted* to beg for

money, goods, or acts of kindness

in any manner whether

verbally, in writing or by act or gesture,

within the area termed the

Eastshire Shopping Centre.

Any such incident will result in the removal of the
individual displaying the behaviour listed herein.

Candidate information 7.4

Eastshire Shopping Centre Policy on Smoking

Policy: 1586
Date: 7 January 2004
Topic: Smoking

Scope

Smoking within the Eastshire Shopping Centre.

Purpose

To prevent individuals smoking.

Action

No individual will be *permitted* to smoke tobacco
or any other substance within the area termed the
Eastshire Shopping Centre.

This includes the use of cigarettes, pipes, cigars
or any other method not referred to here specifically.

Any such incident will result in the removal of the
individual displaying the behaviour listed above.

Role actor's instructions 7

Sandi Smith – Beggars

You are Sandi Smith, a local resident. You have written to the Eastshire Shopping Centre to complain about the beggars who frequent the shopping centre. The beggars (there are two of them) sit on either side of the main entrance, within what can best be described as a wide corridor. One male beggar sits on a cardboard box and the other, a female, sits on a blanket. The male has a dog.

You feel that, although they are not actually approaching individuals for money, the fact that they are there and are asking for money, food and food for the dog makes you feel guilty for not giving. You want them removed from the centre.

Go with the role and think about how you would react to this situation yourself. Ideally, the candidate will have to work to get the information from you.

A role actor will not enter into needless conversation; any talk of the weather or the football results will result in a 'yes' or 'no' and nothing further. If the candidate cannot think of anything to say, simply drop your head and stare at the floor; wait for them to sort themselves out.

Remember that the role actor will normally have a maximum of about 20 lines, so try to keep to this. This means that you will have to be prepared to improvise as you go, without changing the emphasis of the exercise.

What you know that the candidate does not is that some of the security guards are condoning the beggars' behaviour by ignoring some misdemeanours. Since writing your letter of complaint, one of the beggars, the male, has with him a puppy or very small dog. The dog is injured on its side and the man has been asking for money for the vet's bills.

When the candidate enters, say:

'I am Sandi Smith. I have come to see you about the beggars.'

If asked when they are there, say:

'Don't you get out of your office? They are just around the corner; they are there every day.'

This has been ongoing for about two months. If asked what you want done about it, say:

'I want them removed from the shopping centre.'

If the candidate offers a course of action, say:

'Your security guards just walk by them without doing a thing. I have even seen them chatting to the beggars!'

If asked for a description of the security guards, make it up.

If not considered before, ask:

'Is it OK for the beggars to smoke in the shopping centre then?'

Following an explanation in relation to the fact that smoking is not permitted, say:

'But I saw one of the security guards giving them a light just inside the centre. Are they allowed to do this; is it normal procedure?

At an appropriate time, say:

'It seems to me that some of your security guards are treating some people more favourably than others. I see them chatting with the beggars and having a good laugh.'

Later, say:

'It seems to me that you want to get your house in order. You can't have these double standards where the ordinary shoppers are hassled by the beggars and the security guards condone smoking. If I were to light up you would call the fire brigade!'

Finally, add:

'Since I complained, I have noticed that the male beggar has a puppy or small dog; it's hurt on its side. He has been asking for money for the vet's bill. I think this is appalling.'

If the candidate suggests a certain course of action, say:

'Yes, if you think that's best.'

If you are asked for the names of the security guards, you do not have this information.

If asked for a description, invent a character of your choice.

Suggested candidate questions and responses

Role actor: 'Don't you get out of your office? They are just around the corner; they are there every day.'

Your possible responses.

- Thank you, it is important that we identify exactly the individuals you referred to in your letter.

- I have not seen these people myself; would you be kind enough to describe them for me, please?

Role actor: 'I want them removed from the shopping centre.'

- First, may I apologise for the difficulty you have experienced. You can be reassured that no begging will be permitted.

- Having spoken to you, I will ensure that the people begging are identified and spoken to. May I apologise on behalf of the Eastshire Shopping Centre for the distress you have been caused. I will deal with this matter immediately.

Role actor: 'Your security guards just walk by them without doing a thing. I have even seen them chatting to the beggars!'

- Please describe to me in detail what you have seen.

- Please explain exactly what you have witnessed.

Following this account:

- Please accept my apologies if the security guards ignored the begging. You can rest assured that this will not happen again. I will ensure that all security guards are reminded of our policy in relation to begging.

Role actor: 'Is it OK for the beggars to smoke in the shopping centre then?'

- It is not OK; why do you ask?

- No smoking is permitted within the Eastshire Shopping Centre. Have they been smoking?

- Please tell me exactly what is the situation with smoking within the Eastshire Shopping Centre.

Role actor: 'But I saw one of the security guards giving them a light just inside the centre. Are they allowed to do this; is it normal procedure?

- This behaviour is totally unacceptable. Please accept my apologies for this; I will see to it that it never happens again.

- I can assure you that, not only is this not normal procedure, it is also contrary to company policy. Thank you very much for identifying this issue. I will ensure that no such thing happens again.

Further:

- Are you able to describe the security guards you refer to?

Role actor: 'It seems to me that some of your security guards are treating some people more favourably than others. I see them chatting with the beggars and having a good laugh.'

- It appears that some of the security guards are becoming too familiar with these people. I feel that there is a need for further training or a reminder of what is appropriate behaviour.

- Thank you very much for bringing this to my attention.

- Is there a course of action that you would wish me to adopt?

Role actor: 'It seems to me that you want to get your house in order. You can't have these double standards where the ordinary shoppers are hassled by the beggars and the security guards condone smoking. If I were to light up you would call the fire brigade!'

- This situation is unacceptable, I agree. You have my word that positive and swift action will be taken immediately.

- I am sorry you feel that way. I will ensure that this situation is dealt with immediately and that you will not be subjected to either begging or smoking within this centre.

Role actor: 'Since I complained, I have noticed that the male beggar has a puppy or small dog; it's hurt on its side. He has been asking for money for the vet's bill. I think this is appalling.'

- I agree with you; it is in very bad taste. I will contact the RSPCA immediately and take their advice.

- I propose taking advice from the police regarding possible cruelty issues.

- I will pay a visit to the beggars to see the situation for myself. You can be assured that this will be dealt with immediately.

Later, when concluding:

- Thank you again for bringing this to my attention. I am sorry that it has meant that you have had to spend your valuable time speaking to me, but I can assure you that action will be taken to eradicate this problem at once.

- Are there any other issues that you wish to bring to my attention?

Task
In relation to the competencies, list those you consider have been tested in this interactive exercise. The answers are given at the end of this book.

INTERACTIVE EXERCISE 8

Andi Doyle

Exclusion from restaurant

Candidate information

In this exercise there are three pages of information.

1. Memorandum from Ron Moody, Customer Service Manager, Area HQ.
2. Letter of complaint from Andi Doyle.
3. Eastshire Shopping Centre Equal Opportunities Statement.

Following the preparation period, you will be meeting Andi Doyle.

Candidate information 8.1

Memorandum

To: Customer Service Officer, Eastshire Branch
From: Customer Service Manager, Area HQ
Date: Yesterday
Subject: Exclusion from restaurant

Dear Colleague,

I have received a complaint from the person accompanying a group of children, Andi Doyle, in relation to the children being excluded from the Golden Dragon Chinese restaurant. It appears that they attended the restaurant at 1.40 p.m. and were told that they could not enter as there was insufficient time to cook the food within the 20 minutes remaining. The restaurant closes at 2 p.m.

Andi Doyle has been invited to see you today. Please deal with this matter as you see fit.

Ron Moody

Ron Moody

Customer Service Manager, Area HQ

Candidate information 8.2

Letter of complaint from Andi Doyle

Dear Mr Moody,

It is with regret that I have to complain about this issue. You see, the situation is that, last Saturday, I was accompanying a group of children to see the Eastshire Museum. It was our intention to eat at the Golden Dragon Chinese restaurant, the reason being that they have an 'eat all you would like' offer at lunchtime and that appeals to many of our staff!

We were running late, but knew that the restaurant was open until 2 p.m. The group consisted of nine children and three carers, making a total of twelve people. As I entered the restaurant I noticed that it was less than half full, which meant that there was plenty of room for my group. We arrived at 1.40 p.m., so there was still time to eat.

We were quickly approached by a waiter who told me that it was too late for them to cook the food and that it would not be possible for us to stay in the restaurant. I was taken aback, because the food was served at a self-service buffet where people help themselves. I could see no reason why we should not have been allowed to eat there. As you can imagine, the children were both upset and hungry. I would appreciate the opportunity to discuss this matter with you at the earliest opportunity.

Yours sincerely,

Andi Doyle

Andi Doyle

Candidate information 8.3

Eastshire Shopping Centre Equal Opportunities Statement

Policy: 23689
Date: 17 May 2006
Topic: Equal opportunities

The Eastshire Shopping Centre seeks to employ a workforce that reflects the diversity of background and culture within which we operate, and to provide a working environment free from any form of harassment, intimidation, victimisation or unjustifiable discrimination.

We shall treat individuals openly and fairly, and with dignity and respect. We shall value their contribution towards providing a quality service to the people of Eastshire.

All members of the organisation will demonstrate their commitment to these principles and will challenge behaviour that is unacceptable, in particular on the grounds of nationality, gender, race, colour, ethnic or national origin, disability, sexual orientation or marital status.

We shall ensure that our policies and procedures reflect these principles. This applies to all establishments within the Eastshire Shopping Centre.

Role actor's instructions 8

Andi Doyle – Exclusion from restaurant

You are Andi Doyle, a teacher at the Eastshire Community School, a school attended by children with learning difficulties. These include autism, Down's syndrome and various physical and mental disabilities. This was not alluded to in your letter to the candidate.

Last Saturday you were accompanying a group of children to see the Eastshire Museum. It was your intention to eat at the Golden Dragon Chinese restaurant, the reason being that it offers the children the opportunity to try new things to eat. Also, the restaurant has an 'eat all you would like' offer at lunchtime and that appeals to many of the staff!

You were running late, but knew that the restaurant was open until 2 p.m. The group consisted of nine children and three carers, making a total of twelve people. As you entered the restaurant you noticed that it was less than half full, which meant that there was plenty of room for your group.

You were quickly approached by a waiter, whose name badge read 'Dmitri'. He told you that it was too late for the restaurant to cook the food and that it would not be possible for you to stay in the restaurant. You were taken aback because the food was served at a self-service buffet where people help themselves. You could see no reason why you should not have been allowed to eat there. As a consequence, the children were both upset and hungry. You, too, are unhappy about this.

What you know but the candidate does not is that:

- the children have learning difficulties;

- you saw at least four other people entering the restaurant after you had been asked to leave and you could see through the window that they were offered food.

Go with the role and think about how you would react to this situation yourself. Remember though that, within a role play, the acting is never too emotional either with anger or tears. Ideally, the candidate will have to work to get the information from you.

A role actor will not enter into needless conversation; any talk of the weather or the football results will result in a 'yes' or 'no' and nothing further. If the candidate cannot think of anything to say, simply drop your head and stare at the floor; wait for them to sort themselves out.

Remember that the role actor will normally have a maximum of about 20 lines, so try to keep to this. This means that you will have to be prepared to improvise as you go, without changing the emphasis of the exercise.

When the candidate enters, say:

> 'I am Andi Doyle. I am here to see you about the behaviour of the people in the Golden Dragon Chinese restaurant.'

When questioned about this, say:

'It's the fact that we were excluded from the restaurant; the children were hungry.'

If asked to be more specific, say:

'There was plenty of time for us to eat; you see, they serve the food in a buffet style.'

Go on to explain the situation as described above.

At an appropriate stage, say:

'I think this is particularly bad for these children.'

If asked why, say:

'These children have learning difficulties. I think that is the reason they were not allowed to eat there.'

At an appropriate stage, say:

'I feel that seeing the others was just unfair.'

If picked up on, describe the fact that others were allowed into the restaurant and you saw them being seated. (If this is not picked up on, say it again.)

If the candidate suggests a course of action, say:

'Yes, if you think that is best.'

Suggested candidate questions and responses

Role actor: 'I am Andi Doyle. I am here to see you about the behaviour of the people in the Golden Dragon Chinese restaurant.'

Your possible responses.

- Please tell me in detail what happened there.

- Yes, I read your letter with interest. Please describe to me in detail what happened to you and your children.

Role actor: 'It's the fact that we were excluded from the restaurant; the children were hungry.'

- Why was it that you were excluded from the restaurant?

- Did anything in particular happen that would mean the restaurant would not wish to serve you?

- What explanation were you given?

- What happened next?

- Please tell me exactly what was said to you.

Role actor: 'There was plenty of time for us to eat; you see, they serve the food in a buffet style.'

- With the buffet, is there any cooking involved at that time?
- Tell me exactly how much food was left.
- Was there sufficient food to feed your group?

Role actor: 'I think this is particularly bad for these children.'

- What do you mean?
- Why these children in particular?
- What is it about these children that makes it so bad?

Role actor: 'These children have learning difficulties. I think that is the reason they were not allowed to eat there.'

- Explain to me precisely what you mean.
- Please describe to me in detail about your children.
- What effect do these learning difficulties have on the children?
- What makes you feel that this is the reason they were not permitted to eat there?

Role actor: 'I feel that seeing the others was just unfair.'

- What do you mean about the others?
- Please explain to me exactly what you saw.

After hearing about the other people being served, it will be appropriate to state your intentions, e.g.:

- This is inappropriate behaviour; please accept my apologies on behalf of the Eastshire Shopping Centre. I propose speaking to the restaurant immediately. I will keep you fully informed of my progress.

Task
In relation to the competencies, list those you consider have been tested in this interactive exercise. The answers are given at the end of this book.

INTERACTIVE EXERCISE 9

Maninder Johal

Smoking

Candidate information

In this exercise there are four pages of information.

1. Memorandum from Ron Moody, Customer Service Manager, Area HQ.
2. Letter of complaint from Peta/Peter Godley.
3. Eastshire Shopping Centre Policy on Smoking.
4. Building Regulation Proposal from the Polar Bear Air-conditioning Co. Ltd.

Following the preparation period, you will be meeting Maninder Johal.

Candidate information 9.1

Memorandum

To: Customer Service Officer, Eastshire Branch
From: Customer Service Manager, Area HQ
Date: Yesterday
Subject: Smoking

Dear Colleague,

I wish to draw your attention to the fact that a letter of complaint has been received from the owner of the Banshees restaurant, Peta/Peter Godley. The situation is that the air intake for the restaurant's air-conditioning is drawing in smoke. It has been suggested that the smoke is coming from the premises next door, which is the Spear in Hand public house. We have not visited either of the premises to verify the situation; however, I have asked Maninder Johal, who works for the Andean Group, the actual owners of the pub, to attend to discuss this with you today.

I have also included a building regulation application from the Polar Bear Air-conditioning Co. Ltd, which makes interesting reading. Please deal with this as you feel appropriate.

Ron Moody

Ron Moody

Customer Service Manager, Area HQ

Candidate information 9.2

Letter of complaint from Peta/Peter Godley

Dear Mr Moody,

I wish to advise you of a problem I am experiencing within my restaurant. For the last week, my customers have been complaining that they can smell smoke in the premises. Initially, we could not work out where the smell originated, thinking perhaps that the customers were lighting up in the toilets or such like.

Later, we realised that the smoke was actually coming from the pub next door, the Spear in Hand. Due to the change in regulations, the smokers are standing next to our air intake. The result of this is that the restaurant is being filled with smoke. This is unsatisfactory and must be stopped with immediate effect!

Yours sincerely,

P. Godley

P. Godley

Candidate information 9.3

Eastshire Shopping Centre Policy on Smoking

Policy: 3746
Date: 19 July 2008
Topic: Smoking

Scope

Smoking within the Eastshire Shopping Centre.

Purpose

To prevent individuals smoking.

Action

No person shall smoke tobacco or any other tobacco substitute within the confines of the Eastshire Shopping Centre. Those premises benefiting from backing on to the open area may designate an area for smokers in accordance with the 2007 legislation.

Any person found in contravention of this policy will be liable to eviction from the centre.

Candidate information 9.4

Building Regulation Proposal

Polar Bear Air-conditioning Co. Ltd

Re: Banshees restaurant, Eastshire Shopping Centre

Under section 45 of the Eastshire Building Regulations 1993, subsection 15, permission is sought to fully integrate the air-conditioning units that presently exist within the above-named premises. These discrete units will be replaced with one larger unit suitable for the needs of the entire premises.

The environmental impact concerns the location of the air intake, and refrigeration units will be situated next to and be visible to the Spear in Hand public house situated next door. The owners, Andean Group, have been shown the proposed plans and have no objections to this work. It is anticipated that the work will be carried out from the 21st to the 28th of (last month), (this year). All work will be carried out between the hours of 8 a.m. and 8 p.m.

Submitted for your approval,

Glen Mitchell

Glen Mitchell

Role actor's instructions 9

Maninder Johal – Smoking

You are Maninder Johal, who works for the Andean Group, the owners of the Spear in Hand public house. You have been invited to attend to discuss the issue of smoke from the pub being picked up by the air-conditioner in the Banshees restaurant next door.

Since the regulations changed in relation to smoking, in 2007, your customers have been smoking in the approved area, situated outside the premises. Until now you have had no complaints.

You are aware that the air-conditioning unit has been replaced in the restaurant next door. The work was completed very recently.

What you are unaware of (until this is pointed out to you) is the fact that the air intake fan has been positioned so that, when your customers smoke, their smoke is taken into the air-conditioning unit. You feel unwilling to move your smoking area, as the company has spent a considerable amount of money on building, lighting and heating it. You feel that Peta/Peter should have paid more attention to the design of the air-conditioning and looked further than the end of their nose. However, you are open to suggestions from the candidate.

Go with the role and think about how you would react to this situation yourself. Remember though that, within a role play, the acting is never too emotional either with anger or tears. Ideally, the candidate will have to work to get the information from you.

A role actor will not enter into needless conversation; any talk of the weather or the football results will result in a 'yes' or 'no' and nothing further. If the candidate cannot think of anything to say, simply drop your head and stare at the floor; wait for them to sort themselves out.

Remember that the role actor will normally have a maximum of about 20 lines, so try to keep to this. This means that you will have to be prepared to improvise as you go, without changing the emphasis of the exercise.

It is possible that the candidate will approach this in one of two ways.

1. They will not realise that the air-con' was new and will proceed along the lines of the pub being in the wrong.

2. They will realise that the air-con' is new and will request a resolution.

The suggested wording reflects this.

When the candidate enters, say:

> 'I am Maninder Johal. I understand that there is a problem with people smoking in the smoking area of my pub.'

1. Not realising that the air-con' is new and proceeding along the lines of the pub being in the wrong.

When the situation re the smoke entering the premises is pointed out to you, say:

'But the patrons of my pub have been smoking in that area since July 2007; why is there a complaint about them now?'

If questioned regarding the smoke entering the restaurant, say:

'The smoking area has been there for a long time; I would say longer than Peta/Peter's air-conditioning unit.'

If asked what you mean, say:

'Well, we spent a lot of money making the changes for smokers back in 2007. Peta/Peter's air-conditioning was put in last month.'

2. Realising the air-con' is new and requesting a resolution.

When the situation re the smoke entering the premises is pointed out to you, say:

'Yes, I appreciate that the smoke is entering the premises next door, but I would suggest that it is poor planning on their part and not our fault.'

If you are being asked to change the location of the smoking area, say:

'We did not put our smokers by their air intake; it was the other way round.'

If asked to come to a compromise, say:

'This feels very unfair. What is Peta/Peter prepared to do?'

If a suggestion is made, say:

'I suppose I could perhaps look at it again, but I can't guarantee anything.'

Suggested candidate questions and responses

Role actor: 'I am Maninder Johal. I understand that there is a problem with people smoking in the smoking area of my pub.'

1. If you did not realise that the air-con' was new and proceeding along the lines of the pub being in the wrong.

Your possible responses.

- Yes, the situation seems to be that the smoke from your smoking area seems to be going into the air intake of the air-conditioning in the restaurant next door.

- I have received a letter of complaint from Peta/Peter Godley from the Banshees restaurant next door, who is complaining of the smoke from your smoking area entering the air-conditioning.

Role actor: 'But the patrons of my pub have been smoking in that area since July 2007; why is there a complaint about them now?

- I don't know why there is a complaint now.

- Please describe to me in detail the location of your smoking area and their air-conditioning unit.

Role actor: 'The smoking area has been there for a long time; I would say longer than Peta/Peter's air-conditioning unit.'

- Please tell me precisely when your smoking area was built.

- Please tell me precisely when the air-conditioning unit was built.

Role actor: 'Well, we spent a lot of money making the changes for smokers back in 2007. Peta/Peter's air-conditioning was put in last month.'

- I see; so you are saying that the air-conditioning was put in quite recently and in any case a long time after the smoking area.

2. Realising that the air-con' is new and requesting a resolution.

Role actor: 'Yes, I appreciate that the smoke is entering the premises next door, but I would suggest that it is poor planning on their part and not our fault.'

- Explain to me exactly what you mean.

- Poor planning in what way exactly?

- Were you consulted regarding the proposed building plans?

(In relation to changing the location of the smoking area.)

Role actor: 'We did not put our smokers by their air intake; it was the other way round.'

- I appreciate this fact; is there a compromise we can reach?

- I suggest we have a meeting with Peta/Peter and see if we can find a way forward that is mutually beneficial.

(Re the suggestion of a compromise.)

Role actor: 'This feels very unfair. What is Peta/Peter prepared to do?'

- I will contact Peta/Peter and ask for a meeting.

- I cannot speak for Peta/Peter, but will request a meeting with you both as soon as possible.

Role actor: 'I suppose I could perhaps look at it again, but I can't guarantee anything.'

- Thank you for your co-operation in the matter. I feel sure we can work something out.

Task

In relation to the competencies, list those you consider have been tested in this interactive exercise. The answers are given at the end of this book.

INTERACTIVE EXERCISE 10

Les Hanford

Drugs in public toilets

Candidate information

In this exercise there are three pages of information.

1. Memorandum from Ron Moody, Customer Service Manager, Area HQ.
2. Letter of complaint from Jenny Page.
3. Letter of complaint from Brian Townsend.

Following the preparation period, you will be meeting Les Hanford.

Candidate information 10.1

Memorandum

To: Customer Service Officer, Eastshire Branch
From: Customer Service Manager, Area HQ
Date: Yesterday
Subject: The use of drugs in the public toilets

Dear Colleague,

I have received a number of complaints in relation to the state of the toilets next to Starlight's nightclub in the High Street; these are attached for you to read.

The issue appears to be people vomiting in the cubicles and sinks. I am no expert, but I have been told that, if someone takes cocaine after a large amount to drink, they are likely to vomit; they take the cocaine to sober up. Although it is unusual, a syringe has also been found in one of the cubicles. It appears that the problem is emanating from the nightclub next door. Please discuss the matter with Les Hanford, the nightclub manager. I have arranged for you to meet Les today.

Ron Moody

Ron Moody

Customer Service Manager, Area HQ

Candidate information 10.2

Letter of complaint from Jenny Page

Dear Mr Moody,

I am writing to you to complain about the state of the toilets next to Starlight's nightclub. It appears that they are being used to take drugs. I have noticed that there was a syringe left in one of the cubicles. Normally, I would ignore such things, but I nearly stabbed my foot on it as it had been left on the floor. This is an obvious health risk and action must be taken. I know that mothers take their children into the toilets and feel that it is only a matter of time before an accident occurs. I feel that this must be dealt with as soon as possible. Out of interest, I spoke to my daughter about it and she said that the toilets in Starlight's are broken and, apparently, there is a notice on the Gents toilets directing them to use the public toilets outside. I don't think they should be doing this.

Yours sincerely,

Jenny Page

Jenny Page

Candidate information 10.3

Letter of complaint from Brian Townsend

Dear Mr Moody,

As a local resident, I have cause to use the public conveniences on a regular basis. On Wednesday, I went to use the public conveniences that are situated between Starlight's nightclub and the bookshop. The toilets were being unlocked at the time and to my horror, as I entered, I noticed that they were in a terrible state.

There was vomit on the floor and, in some places, on the walls. Fast-food containers were strewn around and a half-eaten kebab had been thrown in the sink. People had obviously been smoking there. I was desperate to use the convenience, but was unable to because of the disgraceful mess. This is simply not good enough.

Yours sincerely,

Brian Townsend

Brian Townsend

Role actor's instructions 10

Les Hanford – Drugs in public toilets

You are Les Hanford, the manager at Starlight's nightclub. You have been called into the office today because a number of complaints have been made in relation to the state of the toilets in the High Street, next to Starlight's.

You are experiencing problems with the maintenance of the toilets in your club. As a result, some of the toilets are not in use. Rather than closing the nightclub, you have put a sign on the Gents toilet directing them to use the public toilets situated just outside.

You are aware that some people use drugs.

Jimmy Starlight has a strict 'no drugs' policy. If people wish to take drugs, they tend to leave the premises to avoid being harassed by the doormen. You are willing to disclose this but in the strictest confidence,

You feel that the public toilets are not your problem.

Go with the role and think about how you would react to this situation yourself. Remember though that, within a role play, the acting is never too emotional either with anger or tears. Ideally, the candidate will have to work to get the information from you.

A role actor will not enter into needless conversation; any talk of the weather or the football results will result in a 'yes' or 'no' and nothing further. If the candidate cannot think of anything to say, simply drop your head and stare at the floor; wait for them to sort themselves out.

Remember that the role actor will normally have a maximum of about 20 lines, so try to keep to this. This means that you will have to be prepared to improvise as you go, without changing the emphasis of the exercise.

When the candidate enters, say:

> 'I am Les Hanford, the manager at Starlight's nightclub.'

If you are questioned why people from the club are using the public toilet, say:

> 'The Gents are out of order in the club.'

If more is asked for, say:

> 'The public Gents are just next door; we put a sign on our Gents to tell men to use them.'

If asked about the drugs, say:

> 'This is strictly in confidence, yes?'

If the candidate agrees, say:

> 'Jimmy Starlight has a strict 'no drugs' policy. If people want to take drugs they have to do so off the premises.'

If asked for more information, say:

'If people want to take drugs, they tend to leave the premises to do it.'

If you are asked what should be done in relation to the problem, say:

'Whatever you think is best.'

Suggested candidate questions and responses

(*Re why people from the club are using the public toilet.*)

Role actor: 'The Gents are out of order in the club.'

Your possible responses.

- Are there any toilet facilities for the gents in your club at present?

- Describe to me exactly the situation regarding the availability of the toilets.

Role actor: 'The public Gents are just next door; we put a sign on our Gents to tell men to use them.'

- You must stop this practice immediately. I will be investigating this situation further and will visit your premises after this interview.

- This is inappropriate. Your licence will be conditional and that includes appropriate toilet facilities.

Role actor: 'This is strictly in confidence, yes?'

- Go on.

- I can't make any promises, but go on.

- What is it you want to say?

Role actor: 'Jimmy Starlight has a strict 'no drugs' policy. If people want to take drugs they have to do so off the premises.'

- What kind of drugs do they take?

- Describe to me in detail the nature of the drug-taking situation.

Role actor: 'If people want to take drugs, they tend to leave the premises to do it.'

- Explain to me where they go to take the drugs.

- Tell me exactly what happens then.

Whether or not the role actor admitted to drugs being taken on the premises, you are aware that there is a drug problem within these premises. However, that is not the issue here. The issue is that the drug-taking has spread to the outside Gents toilets and is now considered to be a problem.

Your responses in relation to this problem could be as follows:

- I propose we visit the club, where we can see the extent of the problem. Following that I will make my recommendations to the local authority in relation to your licence being revoked.

- I recommend that the Gents toilet be fixed at the earliest opportunity. Failure to do this will mean your licence may be revoked.

- The matter of people taking drugs within this establishment has not been an issue. However, your patrons taking drugs in the public toilets is a problem; what do you propose doing about it?

- Both the taking of drugs in this establishment and the fact that your toilets are out of order cause me great concern. I will see to it personally that a report is submitted to the Local Authority and the police. I will not tolerate such things occurring within the centre.

Task
In relation to the competencies, list those you consider have been tested in this interactive exercise. The answers are given at the end of this book.

INTERACTIVE EXERCISE 11

Simran Patel

Lifts

Candidate information

In this exercise there are three pages of information.

1. Memorandum from Ron Moody, Customer Service Manager, Area HQ.
2. Letter of complaint from Corné de Haan.
3. Letter of complaint from Sally Parr.

Following the preparation period, you will be meeting Simran Patel.

Candidate information 11.1

Memorandum

To: Customer Service Officer, Eastshire Branch
From: Customer Service Manager, Area HQ
Date: Yesterday
Subject: Condition of the lifts adjacent to Starlight's nightclub

Dear Colleague,

I have received a number of complaints in relation to the state of the lifts adjacent to Starlight's nightclub; these are attached. The lifts lead from the High Street, next to Starlight's, to the multi-storey car park. The issue appears to be that people are urinating in the lifts. I have visited the lifts myself and I must say they are in a bit of a state.

Please discuss the matter with Simran Patel, the Property Services Manager, whom I have arranged for you to meet today.

Ron Moody

Ron Moody

Customer Service Manager, Area HQ

Candidate information 11.2

Letter of complaint from Corné de Haan

Dear Mr Moody,

I am writing to you to complain about the state of the lifts next to Starlight's nightclub. They are simply disgusting. I am disabled and so have no option but to use the lifts, unlike many of those attending Starlight's, who prefer to use the stairs instead.

I trust you will be dealing with the matter at your earliest convenience.

Yours sincerely,

Corné de Haan

Corné de Haan

Candidate information 11.3

Letter of complaint from Sally Parr

Dear Mr Moody,

I shop regularly within the Eastshire Shopping Centre and park my car in the multi-storey car park. Rather than carrying my heavy shopping up the stairs, I prefer to take the lifts, as I find it more convenient. However, last Monday I walked into one of the lifts and found that someone had obviously been urinating in there. To make it worse, the urine was still in a pool on the floor.

This is unacceptable and I would ask that something be done immediately. Perhaps the nightclub next door would like to contribute to the clean-up, as I understand from my son that it is common practice for some people from that club to use the lifts for the purpose for which they were not intended!

Yours sincerely,

Sally Parr

Sally Parr

Role actor's instructions 11

Simran Patel – Lifts

You are Simran Patel, the Property Services Manager.

You have been called into the office today because a number of complaints have been made in relation to people using the lifts to the multi-storey car park as urinals. You are responsible for ensuring the general upkeep of these lifts and are aware of the fact that they are being used as urinals. What you know, but the candidate does not, is that the underlying reason they are used for this purpose is that the nearby toilets are locked at 8 p.m., when the shops close. This has been done since the management requested that they be closed because people from the nightclub were taking drugs in the cubicles.

Go with the role and think about how you would react to this situation yourself. Remember though that, within a role play, the acting is never too emotional either with anger or tears. Ideally, the candidate will have to work to get the information from you.

A role actor will not enter into needless conversation; any talk of the weather or the football results will result in a 'yes' or 'no' and nothing further. If the candidate cannot think of anything to say, simply drop your head and stare at the floor; wait for them to sort themselves out.

Remember that the role actor will normally have a maximum of about 20 lines, so try to keep to this. This means that you will have to be prepared to improvise as you go, without changing the emphasis of the exercise.

When the candidate enters, say:

'I am Simran Patel, the Property Services Manager. I am here to discuss the state of the lifts with you.'

At an appropriate stage, say:

'The lifts are in a bad state. We are spending a lot of money cleaning them.'

At an appropriate stage, say:

'The situation is that people are using the lifts to urinate in; this occurs only at night-time.'

At an appropriate stage, say:

'It is an unfortunate state of affairs and is due to the reorganisation of the facilities.'

If this is not picked up on, say:

'The decision by the management has meant that we find ourselves cleaning the lifts, which is very costly and time-consuming.'

If it is picked up on, say:

'The toilets are now locked at 8 p.m. by order of the management.'

If asked why, say:

> 'There was a problem with people abusing the nearby public toilets and taking drugs, so the management ordered that they should be locked at 8 p.m.'

At an appropriate time, say:

> 'Now, instead of using the toilets, people are using the lifts and stairwell. Rumour has it that it is the people from the nightclub.'

If a course of action is suggested, say:

> 'Yes, if you think that is best.'

Suggested candidate questions and responses

Role actor: 'I am Simran Patel, the Property Services Manager. I am here to discuss the state of the lifts with you.'

Your possible responses.

- Explain to me in detail about the toilets.
- Describe to me exactly what the situation is.

Role actor: 'The lifts are in a bad state. We are spending a lot of money cleaning them.'

- Tell me about this.
- Describe to me in detail the state of the lifts.
- Explain to me exactly how the money is being spent.

Role actor: 'The situation is that people are using the lifts to urinate in; this occurs only at night-time.'

- Why does this occur only at night?
- What significance does the night have?

Role actor: 'It is an unfortunate state of affairs and is due to the reorganisation of the facilities.'

- What do you mean?
- Describe to me precisely what you mean by the reorganisation of the facilities.
- What is significant about the reorganisation of the facilities?

Role actor: 'The decision by the management has meant that we find ourselves cleaning the lifts, which is very costly and time-consuming.'

- What decision are you referring to?
- Tell me in detail about the management decision.
- How often are you cleaning the lifts?
- What is the cost of the extra cleaning?

Role actor: 'The toilets are now locked at 8 p.m. by order of the management.'

• Why?

• What is the reason for the management closing the lifts at this time?

• Why 8 p.m.?

Role actor: 'There was a problem with people abusing the nearby public toilets and taking drugs, so the management ordered that they should be locked at 8 p.m.'

• I am thinking that it would be more appropriate to open these toilets and have a visible presence of a security guard or a person to look after the toilets.

• I will take personal responsibility for this by organising a security guard to patrol the lift area until such time as I can organise the reopening of the toilets.

Role actor: 'Now, instead of using the toilets, people are using the lifts *and* stairwell. Rumour has it that it is the people from the nightclub.'

• I will visit the nightclub and speak to the owners.

• I am aware that there has been a problem with the facilities and the nightclub.

• Are you responsible for clearing the stairwell also?

It would be appropriate for you to summarise what you have decided or what has been agreed:

• So you are saying that the reason the toilets are in such a state is that you believe people from the nightclub are using the lifts as toilets because the public toilets are locked at 8 p.m. I will visit the nightclub and speak to the owner.

• I would like you to provide me with the exact cost of cleaning the lifts. With this information I can argue for a security guard to patrol the area and prevent further fouling.

Task
In relation to the competencies, list those you consider have been tested in this interactive exercise. The answers are given at the end of this book.

INTERACTIVE EXERCISE 12

Tony/Toni Williamson

Car park

Candidate information

In this exercise there are three pages of information.

1. Memorandum from Ron Moody, Customer Service Manager, Area HQ.
2. Letter from T. Williamson.
3. Letter of complaint from Giles Howard.

Following the preparation period, you will be meeting T. Williamson.

Candidate information 12.1

Memorandum

To: Customer Service Officer, Eastshire Branch
From: Customer Service Manager, Area HQ
Date: Yesterday
Subject: Inappropriate behaviour in the car park

Dear Colleague,

I have received a complaint in relation to the top floor of the multi-storey car park in the High Street. T. Williamson, the car park manager, will be attending to see you today. The complaint is that people are having sex in the car park.

A letter of complaint is also attached.

I know I can rely on you to deal with this matter.

Ron Moody

Ron Moody

Customer Service Manager, Area HQ

Candidate information 12.2

Letter from T. Williamson

Dear Mr Moody,

I am writing to you to ask your advice regarding inappropriate behaviour on the top floor of the car park.

I am responsible for ensuring the car parks are running smoothly, and part of this responsibility includes making sure that people are behaving themselves and that the car parks are clean and tidy.

In this instance, people are not behaving and their mess is leaving the car park untidy and unhygienic. The problem is that, apparently, people are having sex on the top floor of the car park. I have a letter of complaint, which I have attached to this report for your information. Unfortunately, we do not have any CCTV on the top floor.

Yours sincerely,

T. Williamson

T. Williamson

Candidate information 12.3

Letter of complaint from Giles Howard

Dear Eastshire Car Park Services,

I am writing to you to draw your attention to the fact that your car parks are being used for sex. Last night I came home very late and was given a lift to my car, which was parked in the High Street car park.

To my amazement, when I drove on to the top floor I saw about five people engaged in various sexual activities. Fortunately, having seen me, they stopped what they were doing almost immediately. I felt quite awkward as I walked past them to get to my car.

The whole incident has left me feeling uncomfortable about using the car park in future. I know you can't stop people doing what they want to do, but it seems that nothing is being done about this. Where were your security officers?

Please explain to me what you have done to make using the car park a more pleasant experience; for the drivers, that is!

Yours faithfully,

Giles Howard

Giles Howard

Role actor's instructions 12

Tony/Toni Williamson – Car park

You are Toni/Tony Williamson, the car park manager. You have been invited to discuss the problems you are experiencing with people having sex on the top floor of the car park. Giles Howard witnessed them doing this and has complained about it.

Unknown to the role actor, you spoke to Mr Howard on the phone and he told you that the people having sex were all male. You do not like this idea and this will be apparent in your description of what is occurring. Further, he complained about the condoms left lying around the floor.

Go with the role and think about how you would react to this situation yourself. Remember though that, within a role play, the acting is never too emotional either with anger or tears. Ideally, the candidate will have to work to get the information from you.

A role actor will not enter into needless conversation; any talk of the weather or the football results will result in a 'yes' or 'no' and nothing further. If the candidate cannot think of anything to say, simply drop your head and stare at the floor; wait for them to sort themselves out.

Remember that the role actor will normally have a maximum of about 20 lines, so try to keep to this. This means that you will have to be prepared to improvise as you go, without changing the emphasis of the exercise.

When the candidate enters, say:

'I am Toni/Tony Williamson, the car park manager. How can I help you?'

When questioned about the car park incident, say:

'I spoke to Giles Howard on the phone and it's worse than we thought; in fact, they are a bunch of gays.'

If you are challenged as to your choice of words, apologise.

If you are not challenged, continue to describe them as 'bloody gays'.

If you are questioned further, say:

'The problem is that used condoms are being left on the floor; who is responsible for picking them up?'

If you are questioned further, say:

'My staff are not willing to pick up used condoms; it is not in their job description.'

If you are asked what should be done in relation to the problem, say:

'Whatever you think is best.'

Suggested candidate questions and responses

Role actor: 'I am Toni/Tony Williamson, the car park manager. How can I help you?'

Your possible responses.

- I wish to discuss your letter of complaint in relation to people having sex in the car park.

- Please explain to me exactly what the situation is.

Role actor: 'I spoke to Giles Howard on the phone and it's worse then we thought; in fact, they are a bunch of gays.'

If this is not challenged, the role actor is asked to use the term 'bloody gays'.

- I must challenge the way in which you are referring to gay people. This is unacceptable. Please restrict yourself to the terms 'gays' or 'homosexuals'.

- Whether or not they are gay is irrelevant. The situation remains that the car park is being used for activities other than those for which they are intended.

- Tell me in detail the extent of the problem.

- Explain to me the problems this creates from your perspective.

Role actor: 'The problem is that used condoms are being left on the floor; who is responsible for picking them up?'

- Describe to me the extent of the problem.

- What number of condoms are we referring to?

- In answer to your question, if they are treated as litter then the normal services are responsible. However, this issue of safety in the workplace relates to hygiene.

- In the immediate future, I will see to it that a meeting is arranged for all the cleaning staff, where they can be reminded of the safest way to dispose of such items.

Role actor: 'My staff are not willing to pick up used condoms; it is not in their job description.'

- I completely understand your situation. The Eastshire Shopping Centre is more than happy to pay for a specialist company to remove the items.

- I recognise that this aspect of the work is unpleasant and will offer wages at double the normal rate to any person willing to undertake this task.

- I propose that, with immediate effect, security guards are posted to patrol all areas of the car park. It is inappropriate to have sex in the car park.

- Is there anything further I can assist you with?

Task
In relation to the competencies, list those you consider have been tested in this interactive exercise. The answers are given at the end of this book.

INTERACTIVE EXERCISE 13

Dani Gorski

Membership of health club

Candidate information

In this exercise there are three pages of information.

1. Memorandum from Ron Moody, Customer Service Manager, Area HQ.
2. Letter of complaint from Dani Gorski.
3. Eastshire Shopping Centre Equal Opportunities Statement.

Following the preparation period, you will be meeting Dani Gorski.

Candidate information 13.1

Memorandum

To: Customer Service Officer, Eastshire Branch
From: Customer Service Manager, Area HQ
Date: Yesterday
Subject: Membership of the health club

Dear Colleague,

I have received a complaint in relation to the Olympic GB health club (see attached). The allegation appears to be that some members of the Polish community are being excluded from membership of the club.

Dani Gorski, one of the community leaders, is attending today to discuss the matter with you. Please investigate this complaint fully and deal with it in any way you think is appropriate.

Ron Moody

Ron Moody

Customer Service Manager, Area HQ

Candidate information 13.2

Letter of complaint from Dani Gorski

Dear Mr Moody,

I am the community leader for the Polish Association. A number of our members have drawn to my attention the fact that they are unable to join the Olympic GB health club. There appears to be a pattern to this situation, whereby the applicants complete and hand in an application form and then hear nothing further, or they are told that there are no places available at that time.

Those complaining are:

Aniela Duda
Tadeusz Duda
Szczepan Ostrowski
Bronislawa Sokolowska
Doloreta Wosniak
Franciszek Wosniak
Boleslaw Wosniak
Ludmila Adamska
Róza Czerwinska.

As you can see, this is not a one-off. Please can we discuss this matter?

Yours sincerely,

Dani Gorski

Dani Gorski

Candidate information 13.3

Eastshire Shopping Centre Equal Opportunities Statement

Policy: 23689
Date: 17 May 2006
Topic: Equal opportunities

The Eastshire Shopping Centre seeks to employ a workforce that reflects the diversity of background and culture within which we operate, and to provide a working environment free from any form of harassment, intimidation, victimisation or unjustifiable discrimination.

We shall treat individuals openly and fairly, and with dignity and respect. We shall value their contribution towards providing a quality service to the people of Eastshire.

All members of the organisation will demonstrate their commitment to these principles and will challenge behaviour that is unacceptable, in particular on the grounds of nationality, gender, race, colour, ethnic or national origin, disability, sexual orientation or marital status.

We shall ensure that our policies and procedures reflect these principles. This applies to all establishments within the Eastshire Shopping Centre.

Role actor's instructions 13

Dani Gorski – Membership of health club

You are Dani Gorski, a community leader for the Polish Association. You have noticed that there appears to be a problem with Polish people being accepted as members of the Olympic GB health club. There is a distinct pattern to this situation, whereby the applicants complete and hand in an application form and then hear nothing further, or they are told that there are no places available at that time.

Those complaining are:

Aniela Duda
Tadeusz Duda
Szczepan Ostrowski
Bronislawa Sokolowska
Doloreta Wosniak
Franciszek Wosniak
Boleslaw Wosniak
Ludmila Adamska
Róza Czerwinska.

What you know but the role actor does not is that, shortly after Doloreta Wosniak and her family attempted to join, they were told that the club was full, but that they were welcome to join the waiting list. You then submitted a fictitious application in the name of Thomas Malthouse and the application was processed the following week.

Go with the role and think about how you would react to this situation yourself. Remember though that, within a role play, the acting is never too emotional either with anger or tears. Ideally, the candidate will have to work to get the information from you.

A role actor will not enter into needless conversation; any talk of the weather or the football results will result in a 'yes' or 'no' and nothing further. If the candidate cannot think of anything to say, simply drop your head and stare at the floor; wait for them to sort themselves out.

Remember that the role actor will normally have a maximum of about 20 lines, so try to keep to this. This means that you will have to be prepared to improvise as you go, without changing the emphasis of the exercise.

When the candidate enters, say:

> 'I am Dani Gorski. I am here to see you about the problem at the Olympic GB health club.'

When questioned about this, say:

> 'It's as I said in the letter.'

If asked to be more specific, say:

> 'This is racist behaviour. Members of my community are being excluded for no good reason.'

At an appropriate stage, say:

> 'What are you going to do about it?'

At an appropriate stage, say:

> 'I couldn't believe it was happening until the Wosniaks saw me.'

If asked what you mean, say:

> 'Shortly after Doloreta Wosniak and her family attempted to join, they were told that the club was full, but that they were welcome to join the waiting list. I then submitted a fictitious application in the name of Thomas Malthouse and the application was processed the following week! How can this be right?'

If the candidate suggests a course of action, say:

> 'Yes, if you think that is best.'

Suggested candidate questions and responses

Role actor: 'I am Dani Gorski. I am here to see you about the problem at the Olympic GB health club.'

Your possible responses.

- Please describe to me in detail the extent of the problem.
- Please describe to me in detail what the situation is.

Role actor: 'This is racist behaviour. Members of my community are being excluded for no good reason.'

- Please tell me in detail about the racist element of your situation.
- Describe to me exactly how members of your community are being excluded.

Role actor: 'What are you going to do about it?'

- I will take personal responsibility to get to the root of this situation.
- I have a number of options:
  - I can speak to the health club and identify any misunderstandings;
  - I can speak to the health club's head office;
  - I can consider any training needs.

Role actor: 'I couldn't believe it was happening until the Wosniaks saw me.'

- What do you mean?
- Describe to me exactly what happened in relation to the Wosniaks.

Role actor: 'Shortly after Doloreta Wosniak and her family attempted to join, they were told that the club was full, but that they were welcome to join the waiting list. I then submitted a fictitious application in the name of Thomas Malthouse and the application was processed the following week! How can this be right?'

- This situation cannot and will not be tolerated. I find it offensive and the Eastshire Shopping Centre has an equal opportunities policy in relation to such behaviour.

- I will take personal responsibility to ensure that this is rectified immediately.

- In light of the situation, what outcome do the members of your community want?

- Is there any other matter that I should be aware of?

Task

In relation to the competencies, list those you consider have been tested in this interactive exercise. The answers are given at the end of this book.

INTERACTIVE EXERCISE 14

Amandeep Phool

Lateness

Candidate information

In this exercise there are three pages of information.

1. Memorandum from Ron Moody, Customer Service Manager, Area HQ.
2. Duty roster for Amandeep Phool.
3. Memorandum from the Quality Control Department.

Following the preparation period, you will be meeting Amandeep Phool.

Candidate information 14.1

Memorandum

To: Customer Service Officer, Eastshire Branch
From: Customer Service Manager, Area HQ
Date: Yesterday
Subject: Lateness

Dear Colleague,

I wish to draw your attention to the fact that a customer service assistant, Amandeep Phool, has been regularly late for the past two months. The lateness has been increasing during the last month. Further, Amandeep is taking the odd day off here and there, to such an extent that the allocated annual leave is insufficient to cover the next summer holiday. You will find a report outlining the lateness and use of leave attached.

I would like you to speak to Amandeep about the lateness. Further, I would like to know how having two weeks off in the summer will be possible now that the leave has been used up. Deal with this as you see fit.

Ron Moody

Ron Moody

Customer Service Manager, Area HQ

Candidate information 14.2

Duty roster for Amandeep Phool

1 July	Wed.	Leave	AL	1 August	Sat.		Off
2 July	Thu.	Late 8.30	6–2	2 August	Sun.		Off
3 July	Fri.	Leave	AL	3 August	Mon.	Late 3.00	2–10
4 July	Sat.		Off	4 August	Tue.		2–10
5 July	Sun.		Off	5 August	Wed.	Leave	AL
6 July	Mon.		2–10	6 August	Thu.		2–10
7 July	Tue.		2–10	7 August	Fri.	Late 5.00	2–10
8 July	Wed.	Leave	AL	8 August	Sat.		Off
9 July	Thu.		2–10	9 August	Sun.		Off
10 July	Fri.		2–10	10 August	Mon.		6–2
11 July	Sat.		Off	11 August	Tue.		6–2
12 July	Sun.		Off	12 August	Wed.	Leave	AL
13 July	Mon.	Late 7.30	6–2	13 August	Thu.		6–2
14 July	Tue.		6–2	14 August	Fri.	Late 6.30	6–2
15 July	Wed.	Leave	AL	15 August	Sat.		Off
16 July	Thu.	Leave	AL	16 August	Sun.		Off
17 July	Fri.	Leave	AL	17 August	Mon.		2–10
18 July	Sat.		Off	18 August	Tue.		2–10
19 July	Sun.		Off	19 August	Wed.	Leave	AL
20 July	Mon.	Leave	AL	20 August	Thu.		2–10
21 July	Tue.	Late 2.15	2–10	21 August	Fri.	Late 3.30	2–10
22 July	Wed.	Leave	AL	22 August	Sat.		Off
23 July	Thu.		2–10	23 August	Sun.		Off
24 July	Fri.		2–10	24 August	Mon.		6–2
25 July	Sat.		Off	25 August	Tue.		6–2
26 July	Sun.		Off	26 August	Wed.	Leave	AL
27 July	Mon.	Leave	AL	27 August	Thu.	Late 6.30	6–2
28 July	Tue.	Leave	AL	28 August	Fri.		6–2
29 July	Wed.	Leave	AL	29 August	Sat.		Off
30 July	Thu.	Leave	AL	30 August	Sun.		Off
31 July	Fri.	Leave	AL	31 August	Mon.	Late 3.00	2–10

Figures for July and August:
AL = Annual leave = 17 days
Late on 9 occasions

Candidate information 14.3

Memorandum from the Quality Control Department

To: Ron Moody, Customer Service Manager, Area HQ
From: Ali Smith, Quality Control Department
Date: Yesterday
Topic: Amandeep Phool, lateness

Ron,

It looks like you have a problem here. The computer system shows that Amandeep Phool is in need of attention. I must say, a lot of leave has certainly been taken!

Only thing is, this lateness is far too high – three days in July, which by company standards is just about OK, but six in August!? I think it's time to have words.

All the best,

Ali

Role actor's instructions 14

Amandeep Phool – Lateness

You are Amandeep Phool, a customer service assistant. You have been invited to the meeting to discuss the issue of your lateness and the fact that you are quickly using up your annual leave. The truth of the situation is that you are a carer; your partner has multiple sclerosis (MS). You are reliant upon friends and family to help you and money is short, and this is making you very anxious. You are using the annual leave because you cannot find anyone to cover for you.

Go with the role and think about how you would react to this situation yourself. Remember though that, within a role play, the acting is never too emotional either with anger or tears. Ideally, the candidate will have to work to get the information from you.

A role actor will not enter into needless conversation; any talk of the weather or the football results will result in a 'yes' or 'no' and nothing further. If the candidate cannot think of anything to say, simply drop your head and stare at the floor; wait for them to sort themselves out.

Remember that the role actor will normally have a maximum of about 20 lines, so try to keep to this. This means that you will have to be prepared to improvise as you go, without changing the emphasis of the exercise.

When the candidate enters, say:

'I am Amandeep Phool; you wanted to see me?'

At an appropriate stage, apologise and say:

'I am sorry about the lateness.'

If questioned about the amount of annual leave you have taken, say:

'It's my annual leave, so I can do what I want with it, can't I?'

If pushed on the subject, become slightly defensive and say:

'Look, it's my time off, my annual leave and sometimes I am late, but I will make it up to you. It's my life and I am doing the best I can.'

Later, let drop:

'It's the situation, that's all.'

If questioned on this, say:

'It's my partner.'

If asked what you mean, give the account about you being a carer for your partner who has multiple sclerosis (MS).

If asked about the leave before the lateness, say:

'I need Wednesdays off.'

If asked why, say:

'You would do, too, in my position.'

If they pick up on this, explain all.

If they ask what you would like in the way of help, say:

'I don't know.'

Go along with any suggestions they may have for you by saying:

'Yes, if you think that is best.'

Suggested candidate questions and responses

1. In respect of the issue of lateness.

Role actor: 'I am sorry about the lateness.'

Your possible responses.

- Why are you so often late?

- Yes, it has been brought to my attention. Is there a reason for this?

- I notice you have been late for work on nine occasions within the last two months. Is there a reason for this?

- Please describe to me exactly why you have been late on so many occasions recently.

Role actor: 'It's my annual leave, so I can do what I want with it, can't I?'

- Yes, it is your annual leave and you are at liberty to take it at the company's discretion.

- We are concerned that the annual leave you have taken to date will jeopardise your summer holiday leave.

- You have run out of annual leave, so what are you going to do about your summer leave?

- I am concerned that there may be something wrong that you are not sharing with us. Why are you taking so much annual leave and time off?

- Please explain to me in detail the reason for you taking so much time off and annual leave.

Role actor: 'Look, it's my time off, my annual leave and sometimes I am late, but I will make it up to you. It's my life and I am doing the best I can.'

- Yes, I do appreciate this, but there appears to be a problem. What is the matter?

- It is your personal life that troubles me. What is the problem?

- It appears that your personal life is encroaching into your work life. I am here to help you if you will let me. How can I help you?

Role actor: 'It's the situation, that's all.'

- Tell me about that.
- What situation is that exactly?
- Describe to me in detail your situation.
- Tell me precisely what you mean.

Role actor: 'It's my partner.'

- What is the situation with your partner?
- Is there a problem?
- Is there something I can help you with?
- Tell me about that.

2. In respect of the issue of leave.

To introduce the topic you could say:

- I see from your duty roster that, during July and August, you have taken 17 days of your annual leave. Why is this?

Role actor: 'I need Wednesdays off.'

- Why is this?
- Why do you need Wednesdays off?
- But it is not just Wednesdays that you have been taking off, I notice.

Role actor: 'You would do, too, in my position.'

- What position is that?
- Tell me precisely what you mean.

Following the account about the role actor being a carer for their partner, who has MS, you would be expected to make suggestions as to how to deal with this problem. You can consider the following:

- What can I do to assist you?
- Is there anything I can do?

In this exercise the role actor was directed not to ask for anything in particular, in which case you will be expected to make some suggestions, e.g.:

- I will take personal responsibility for this matter. I propose we consider your needs in detail and discuss how we can accommodate you.
- What I believe is needed is a more flexible shift pattern aimed at meeting your specific needs. I will see to it personally that this is done.

Task

In relation to the competencies, list those you consider have been tested in this interactive exercise. The answers are given at the end of the book.

INTERACTIVE EXERCISE 15

Terri Townsend

Harassment

Candidate information

In this exercise there are three pages of information.

1. Memorandum from Ron Moody, Customer Service Manager, Area HQ.
2. Eastshire Shopping Centre Equal Opportunities Statement.
3. Letter of complaint from Terri Townsend.

Following the preparation period, you will be meeting Terri Townsend.

Candidate information 15.1

Memorandum

To: Customer Service Officer, Eastshire Branch
From: Customer Service Manager, Area HQ
Date: Yesterday
Subject: Overly-familiar security guard

Dear Colleague,

I wonder if you could deal with the attached. It is a letter of complaint from a Terri Townsend, who has an issue with one of our security guards. It appears they are being overly familiar, which is causing annoyance.

I have invited Terri to discuss the matter with you. Please deal with this situation in the way you feel is the most appropriate. Just in case, I have attached our Equal Opportunities Statement for your information.

Ron Moody

Ron Moody

Customer Service Manager, Area HQ

Candidate information 15.2

Eastshire Shopping Centre Equal Opportunities Statement

Policy: 23689
Date: 17 May 2006
Topic: Equal opportunities

The Eastshire Shopping Centre seeks to employ a workforce that reflects the diversity of background and culture within which we operate, and to provide a working environment free from any form of harassment, intimidation, victimisation or unjustifiable discrimination.

We shall treat individuals openly and fairly, and with dignity and respect. We shall value their contribution towards providing a quality service to the people of Eastshire.

All members of the Eastshire Shopping Centre will demonstrate their commitment to these principles and will challenge behaviour that is unacceptable, in particular on the grounds of nationality, gender, race, colour, ethnic or national origin, disability, sexual orientation or marital status.

We shall ensure that our policies and procedures reflect these principles. This applies to all establishments within the Eastshire Shopping Centre.

Candidate information 15.3

Letter of complaint from Terri Townsend

Dear Sir,

I am a schoolteacher from Oakway Junior School. I shop regularly within the Eastshire Shopping Centre, as it is close to my school and, as such, is convenient to get to during the lunch break. Recently, the behaviour of one of the security guards has begun to cause me distress. The individual tries to speak to me on every occasion they see me. The person actually stands in my way, so that I am forced to stop, and asks me questions that I find intrusive and irritating; they attempt to be funny, but I find this sense of humour silly.

I wish I hadn't spoken on the first occasion we met, but I didn't want to appear rude. Now I have had enough and want the behaviour to stop. The security guard has not taken the hint, as I have tried to ignore them, and so I am writing to you to complain. The name badge displayed reads E. Durdin. I trust you will give this letter the most appropriate and urgent attention.

Yours faithfully,

Terri Townsend

Terri Townsend

Role actor's instructions 15

Terri Townsend – Harassment

You are Terri Townsend, a local schoolteacher. You shop regularly within the Eastshire Shopping Centre, as it is close to your school, and as you find it convenient to get to during the lunch break. However, recently one of the security guards has taken it upon themselves to speak to you on every occasion that you pass by.

The security guard actually stands in your way so that you are forced to stop. You find the questioning increasingly intrusive and irritating. The security guard attempts to be funny, but you find the sense of humour silly.

You wish you hadn't responded on the first occasion you met, but you didn't want to appear rude. Now you have had enough and want the behaviour to stop. The security guard has not taken the hint, as you have tried to ignore this behaviour, and so you are attending today to complain.

What you know but the candidate does not is that things have progressed further since the letter of complaint was received. The guard approached you yesterday afternoon and handed you an envelope. Without thinking, you took it. You later opened it and found inside a picture of the guard in uniform, but it was undone and very suggestive. With it was a letter expressing the guard's desire for you and providing a telephone number and e-mail address. Without thinking, you have burned both the photograph and the letter. The situation has made you unhappy and unsure of what to do next.

Further to this, you were sexually assaulted less than a year ago. Although reported to the police, you received no professional counselling. These recent incidents are very similar in nature to the previous assault and affect your behaviour.

Go with the role and think about how you would react to this situation yourself. Ideally, the candidate will have to work to get the information from you.

A role actor will not enter into needless conversation; any talk of the weather or the football results will result in a 'yes' or 'no' and nothing further. If the candidate cannot think of anything to say, simply drop your head and stare at the floor; wait for them to sort themselves out.

Remember that the role actor will normally have a maximum of about 20 lines, so try to keep to this. This means that you will have to be prepared to improvise as you go, without changing the emphasis of the exercise.

The security guard is E. Durdin, aged about 20 years, and is 5 ft 10 in., with several piercings in both ears, and is clean shaven with (in your opinion) a modern messy hairstyle.

When the candidate enters, say:

'I am Terri Townsend. I am here to see you about the security guard.'

First, explain the contents of your letter, no more.

If asked what has happened, say:

'It's just as I said in the letter.'

If asked what you want done about this, say:

'I just want the guard to stop hassling me. This has been going on for about three months.'

At an appropriate time, say:

'I can't believe that, in this day and age, people think they can hassle people in this way. Don't you give your guards training?'

When appropriate, say:

'Don't you have a policy on things like this?'

Wait until the candidate offers an appropriate course of action and then explain about the letter and photograph – remember that you no longer have these.

At an appropriate time, say:

'I am afraid to come into the Shopping Centre. I saw the guard there the other day and I thought I was going to be sick.'

At an appropriate time, ask:

'What are you going to do? The guard is working here today.'

Finally, say:

'It's like it's happening all over again.'

If asked what you mean, say:

'I was sexually assaulted a while ago. I don't want to go into any detail about it, but this feels just like it is happening again and I don't think I can cope any more.'

As a result of the assault, you received no professional counselling and feel increasingly unable to deal with certain situations in your life.

If the candidate suggests a certain course of action, say:

'Yes, if you think that's best.'

Suggested candidate questions and responses

Role actor: 'I just want the guard to stop hassling me. This has been going on for about three months.'

Your possible responses.

- In what way exactly have you been hassled?
- Please describe to me exactly what has been happening.
- Start at the very beginning. What has happened exactly?

Or a more empathic response could begin with:

- First, let me assure you that coming here to discuss this matter with me was a very sensible thing to do. Please accept my sincerest apologies and let me assure you that the situation will stop immediately.

Role actor: 'I can't believe that, in this day and age, people think they can hassle people in this way. Don't you give your guards training?'

- I can assure you that the security guards have been trained and that is my concern. This individual knows that this behaviour is wrong. I can assure you I will investigate this matter thoroughly.

- They are trained and I am considering attending that training to see exactly what it entails. If it transpires that the training is insufficient, I will ensure that something is done about it.

Role actor: 'Don't you have a policy on things like this?'

- There is a policy on this (*read out the Equal Opportunities Statement*). It is clear to me that this individual is in breach of this policy.

- There is a policy in relation to the situation you are experiencing and it includes the need to '. . . provide a working environment free from any form of harassment, intimidation, victimisation or unjustifiable discrimination'. Clearly this person is in breach of this policy.

- I can either recommend some form of discipline or, alternatively, a course of training. Do you have a preference?

Following the explanation regarding the letter and photograph:

- Again, please accept my apologies. This behaviour is not acceptable.

- Is there anything the Eastshire Shopping Centre can do to help you?

- Clearly, you have been troubled by this situation. I would like to offer you some shopping tokens by way of an apology.

- Do you have a copy of the letter or the photograph?

- What happened to the letter and the photograph?

- Did you show these to any other person?

Role actor: 'I am afraid to come into the Shopping Centre. I saw the guard there the other day and I thought I was going to be sick.'

- I am sorry you feel this way. What can I do to assist you?

Role actor: 'What are you going to do? The guard is working here today.'

- I will escort you to wherever you wish to go.

- Would you like me to escort you through the Shopping Centre and back to wherever you are going?

- I will speak to the security guard as soon as possible. This behaviour cannot continue.

- Thank you for bringing this to my attention. Is there anything further I can assist you with?

Role actor: 'It's like it's happening all over again.'

- What is happening again?

- What do you mean?

Role actor: 'I was sexually assaulted a while ago. I don't want to go into any detail about it, but this feels just like it is happening again and I don't think I can cope any more.'

- That sounds like a horrific experience for you. Is there anything I can do to help?

- I am sorry to hear that. Is there anyone I can put you in contact with to help you?

Task

In relation to the competencies, list those you consider have been tested in this interactive exercise. The answers are given at the end of this book.

Appendix A

Core competencies mapped against the Interactive Exercises

No	Name	Subject	Competencies considered (see Appendix B)
1	Nat Emerson	Homophobic bullying at work	1. Respect for race and diversity 3. Community and customer focus 4. Effective communication 5. Problem solving 6. Personal responsibility
2	Jo Chi	Gay bar	1. Respect for race and diversity 4. Effective communication 5. Problem solving
3	Muhtarem Mustafa	Halal shop	1. Respect for race and diversity 4. Effective communication 5. Problem solving 6. Personal responsibility
4	Peta/Peter Godley	Rats in the restaurant	3. Community and customer focus 4. Effective communication 5. Problem solving
5	Rennie Chandler	Assistance refused	1. Respect for race and diversity 3. Community and customer focus 4. Effective communication 5. Problem solving 6. Personal responsibility
6	Jordan Rose	Bad language	1. Respect for race and diversity 3. Community and customer focus 4. Effective communication 5. Problem solving 6. Personal responsibility 7. Resilience
7	Sandi Smith	Beggars	1. Respect for race and diversity 4. Effective communication 5. Problem solving 6. Personal responsibility 7. Resilience
8	Andi Doyle	Exclusion from restaurant	1. Respect for race and diversity 4. Effective communication 5. Problem solving 6. Personal responsibility
9	Maninder Johal	Smoking	3. Community and customer focus 4. Effective communication 5. Problem solving 6. Personal responsibility
10	Les Hanford	Drugs in public toilets	3. Community and customer focus 4. Effective communication 5. Problem solving

No	Name	Subject	Competencies considered (see Appendix B)
11	Simran Patel	Lifts	4. Effective communication 5. Problem solving 6. Personal responsibility
12	Tony/Toni Williamson	Car park	1. Respect for race and diversity 4. Effective communication 5. Problem solving 6. Personal responsibility
13	Dani Gorski	Membership of health club	1. Respect for race and diversity 4. Effective communication 5. Problem solving 6. Personal responsibility
14	Amandeep Phool	Lateness	1. Respect for race and diversity 4. Effective communication 5. Problem solving 6. Personal responsibility 7. Resilience
15	Terri Townsend	Harassment	1. Respect for race and diversity 3. Community and customer focus 4. Effective communication 5. Problem solving 6. Personal responsibility

Appendix B

National Core Competencies

Reproduced in part, with kind permission, from *The Integrated Competency Behavioural Framework Version 9.0 (May 2007)* by Skills for Justice.

1. Respect for race and diversity — Considers and shows respect for the opinions, circumstances and feelings of colleagues and members of the public, no matter what their race, religion, position, background, circumstances, status or appearance.

Required level — Understands other people's views and takes them into account. Is tactful and diplomatic when dealing with people. Treats them with dignity and respect at all times. Understands and is sensitive to social, cultural and racial differences.

- Sees issues from other people's viewpoints.

- Is polite, tolerant and patient with people inside and outside the organisation, treating them with respect and dignity.

- Respects the needs of everyone involved when sorting out disagreements.

- Shows understanding and sensitivity to people's problems and vulnerabilities.

- Deals with diversity issues and gives positive practical support to staff who may feel vulnerable.

- Listens to and values others' views and opinions.

- Uses language in an appropriate way and is sensitive to the way it may affect people.

- Acknowledges and respects a broad range of social and cultural customs and beliefs and values within the law.

- Understands what offends others and adapts own actions accordingly.

- Respects and maintains confidentiality, where appropriate.

- Delivers difficult messages sensitively.

- Challenges attitudes and behaviour which are abusive, aggressive or discriminatory.

- Takes into account others' personal needs and interests.

- Supports minority groups both inside and outside their organisation.

Negative indicators

- Does not consider other people's feelings.

- Does not encourage people to talk about personal issues.

- Criticises people without considering their feelings and motivation.

- Makes situations worse with inappropriate remarks, language or behaviour.

- Is thoughtless and tactless when dealing with people.

- Is dismissive and impatient with people.

- Does not respect confidentiality.

- Unnecessarily emphasises power and control in situations where this is not appropriate.

- Intimidates others in an aggressive and overpowering way.

- Uses humour inappropriately.

- Shows bias and prejudice when dealing with people.

2. Team working   Develops strong working relationships inside and outside the team to achieve common goals. Breaks down barriers between groups and involves others in discussions and decisions.

Required level   Works effectively as a team member and helps build relationships within it. Actively helps and supports others to achieve team goals.

- Understands own role in a team.

- Actively supports and assists the team to reach their objectives.

- Is approachable and friendly to others.

- Makes time to get to know people.

- Co-operates with and supports others.

- Offers to help other people.

- Asks for and accepts help when needed.

- Develops mutual trust and confidence in others.

- Willingly takes on unpopular or routine tasks.

- Contributes to team objectives no matter what the direct personal benefit may be.

- Acknowledges that there is often a need to be a member of more than one team.

- Takes pride in their team and promotes their team's performance to others.

Negative indicators

- Does not volunteer to help other team members.

- Is only interested in taking part in high-profile and interesting activities.

- Takes credit for success without recognising the contribution of others.

- Works to own agenda rather than contributing to team performance.

- Allows small exclusive groups of people to develop.

- Plays one person off against another.

- Restricts and controls what information is shared.

- Does not let people say what they think.

- Does not offer advice or get advice from others.

- Shows little interest in working jointly with other groups to meet the goals of everyone involved.

- Does not discourage conflict within the organisation.

3. Community and customer focus	Focuses on the customer and provides a high-quality service that is tailored to meet their individual needs. Understands the communities that are served and shows an active commitment to policing that reflects their needs and concerns.
Required level	Provides a high level of service to customers. Maintains contact with customers, works out what they need and responds to them.

- Presents an appropriate image to the public and other organisations.

- Supports strategies that aim to build an organisation that reflects the community it serves.

- Focuses on the customer in all activities.

- Tries to sort out customers' problems as quickly as possible.

- Apologises when they are at fault or have made mistakes.

- Responds quickly to customer requests.

- Makes sure that customers are satisfied with the service they receive.

- Manages customer expectations.

- Keeps customers updated on progress.

- Balances customer needs with organisational needs.

Negative indicators

- Is not customer focused and does not consider individual needs.
- Does not tell customers what is going on.
- Presents an unprofessional image to customers.
- Only sees a situation from their own view, not from the customer's view.
- Shows little interest in the customer – only deals with their immediate problem.
- Does not respond to the needs of the local community.
- Focuses on organisational issues rather than customer needs.
- Does not make the most of opportunities to talk to people in the community.
- Slow to respond to customers' requests.
- Fails to check that the customers' needs have been met.

4. Effective communication	Communicates ideas and information effectively, both verbally and in writing. Uses language and a style of communication that is appropriate to the situation and people being addressed. Makes sure others understand what is going on.
Required level	Communicates all needs, instructions and decisions clearly. Adapts the style of communication to meet the needs of the audience. Checks for understanding.

- Deals with issues directly.
- Clearly communicates needs and instructions.
- Clearly communicates management decisions and policy, and the reasons behind them.
- Communicates face to face wherever possible and if appropriate.
- Speaks with authority and confidence.
- Changes the style of communication to meet the needs of the audience.
- Manages group discussions effectively.
- Summarises information to check people understand it.
- Supports arguments and recommendations effectively in writing.
- Produces well-structured reports and written summaries.

Negative indicators

- Is hesitant, nervous and uncertain when speaking.
- Speaks without first thinking through what to say.

- Uses inappropriate language or jargon.

- Speaks in a rambling way.

- Does not consider the target audience.

- Avoids answering difficult questions.

- Does not give full information without being questioned.

- Writes in an unstructured way.

- Uses poor spelling, punctuation and grammar.

- Assumes others understand what has been said without actually checking.

- Does not listen and interrupts at inappropriate times.

5. Problem solving   Gathers information from a range of sources. Analyses information to identify problems and issues, and makes effective decisions.

Required level   Gathers enough relevant information to understand specific issues and events. Uses information to identify problems and draw conclusions. Makes good decisions.

- Identifies where to get information and gets it.

- Gets as much information as is appropriate on all aspects of a problem.

- Separates relevant information from irrelevant information and important information from unimportant information.

- Takes on information quickly and accurately.

- Reviews all the information gathered to understand the situation and to draw logical conclusions.

- Identifies and links causes and effects.

- Identifies what can and cannot be changed.

- Takes a systematic approach to solving problems.

- Remains impartial and avoids jumping to conclusions.

- Refers to procedures and precedents, as necessary, before making decisions.

- Makes good decisions that take account of all relevant factors.

Negative indicators

- Doesn't deal with problems in detail and does not identify underlying issues.

- Does not gather enough information before coming to conclusions.

- Does not consult other people who may have extra information.

- Does not research background.

- Shows no interest in gathering or using intelligence.
- Does not gather evidence.
- Makes assumptions about the facts of a situation.
- Does not recognise problems until they have become significant issues.
- Gets stuck in the detail of complex situations and cannot see the main issues.
- Reacts without considering all the angles.
- Becomes distracted by minor issues.

6. Personal responsibility	Takes personal responsibility for making things happen and achieving results. Displays motivation, commitment, perseverance and conscientiousness. Acts with a high degree of integrity.
Required level	Takes personal responsibility for own actions and for sorting out issues or problems that arise. Is focused on achieving results to required standards and developing skills and knowledge.

- Accepts personal responsibility for own decisions and actions.
- Takes action to resolve problems and fulfil own responsibilities.
- Keeps promises and does not let colleagues down.
- Takes pride in work.
- Is conscientious in completing work on time.
- Follows things through to satisfactory conclusion.
- Displays initiative, taking on tasks without having to be asked.
- Is self-motivated, showing enthusiasm and dedication to their role.
- Focuses on task even if it is routine.
- Improves own professional knowledge and keeps it up to date.
- Is open, honest and genuine, standing up for what is right.
- Makes decisions based upon ethical consideration and organisational integrity.

Negative indicators

- Passes responsibility upwards inappropriately.
- Is not concerned about letting others down.
- Will not deal with issues, just hopes they will go away.
- Blames others rather than admitting to mistakes or looking for help.

- Is unwilling to take on responsibility.
- Puts in the minimum effort that is needed to get by.
- Shows a negative and disruptive attitude.
- Shows little energy and enthusiasm for work.
- Expresses a cynical attitude to the organisation and their job.
- Gives up easily when faced with problems.
- Fails to recognise personal weaknesses and development needs.
- Makes little or no attempt to develop self or keep up to date.

7. Resilience   Shows resilience, even in difficult circumstances. Is prepared to make difficult decisions and has the confidence to see them through.

Required level   Shows reliability and resilience in difficult circumstances. Remains calm and confident, and responds logically and decisively in difficult situations.

- Is reliable in a crisis, remains calm and thinks clearly.
- Sorts out conflict and deals with hostility and provocation in a calm and restrained way.
- Responds to challenges rationally, avoiding inappropriate emotion.
- Deals with difficult emotional issues and then moves on.
- Manages conflicting pressures and tensions.
- Maintains professional ethics when confronted with pressure from others.
- Copes with ambiguity and deals with uncertainty and frustration.
- Resists pressure to make quick decisions where consideration is needed.
- Remains focused and in control of situation.
- Makes and carries through decisions, even though they are unpopular, difficult or controversial.
- Stands firmly by a position when it is right to do so.
- Defends their staff from excessive criticisms from outside the team.

Negative indicators

- Gets easily upset, frustrated and annoyed.
- Panics and becomes agitated when problems arise.
- Walks away from confrontation when it would be more appropriate to get involved.
- Needs constant reassurance, support and supervision.
- Uses inappropriate physical force.

137

- Gets too emotionally involved in situations.

- Reacts inappropriately when faced with rude or abusive people.

- Deals with situations aggressively.

- Complains and whinges about problems rather than dealing with them.

- Gives in inappropriately when under pressure.

- Worries about making mistakes and avoids difficult situations wherever possible.

Index